Jens Peter Brune,
Dieter Krohn (Eds.)

Socratic Dialogue and Ethics

D0913520

Sokratisches Philosophieren

Schriftenreihe der
Philosophisch-Politischen Akademie (PPA)
und der
Gesellschaft für Sokratisches Philosophieren (GSP)

Series on Socratic Philosophizing

of the Philosophical-Political Academy (PPA)
and the Society of Socratic Facilitators (GSP)

herausgegeben von/edited by

Dieter Krohn, Barbara Neißer, Nora Walter †

Band/Volume IX

LIT

Jens Peter Brune, Dieter Krohn (Eds.)

SOCRATIC DIALOGUE
AND ETHICS

LIT

Bibliographic information published by Die Deutsche Bibliothek
Die Deutsche Bibliothek lists this publication in the Deutsche
Nationalbibliografie; detailed bibliographic data are available in the
Internet at http://dnb.ddb.de.

ISBN 3-8258-6309-3

A catalogue record for this book is available from the British library

© LIT VERLAG Münster   2005
Grevener Str./Fresnostr. 2   48159 Münster
Tel. 0251-62 03 20   Fax 0251-23 19 72
e-Mail: lit@lit-verlag.de   http://www.lit-verlag.de

Distributed in North America by:

Transaction Publishers
New Brunswick (U.S.A.) and London (U.K.)

Transaction Publishers   Tel.: (732) 445 - 2280
Rutgers University   Fax: (732) 445 - 3138
35 Berrue Circle   for orders (U. S. only):
Piscataway, NJ 08854   toll free (888) 999 - 6778

Contents

Reports

Dieter Krohn

Welcome to the Third International Conference on the Socratic Dialogue — And a Short Introduction to the Socratic Method

In 1996, the Society for the Furtherance of Critical Philosophy, supported by the Philosophisch-Politische Akademie, organised the First International Conference on the Socratic Dialogue, which was held in Hillcroft College near London. Participants mainly from Great Britain, the Netherlands and Germany met to engage in Socratic Dialogue and to discuss topics of the Critical Philosophy.

Two years later the Dutch Socratics, supported by the Society for the Furtherance of Critical Philosophy and the Philosophisch-Politische Akademie, organised the Second International Conference on the Socratic Dialogue, which took place in Leusden near Amersfoort. The emphasis was on the Dutch Experience, the application of the Socratic Dialogue in different forms and, amongst others, in the context of business consultancy. The number of participants and the number of nationalities present had increased.

Two years later again, in the year 2000, after some decades of Socratic Dialogue in the tradition of Leonard Nelson and Gustav Heckmann in Germany, we are meeting in Loccum to attend the Third International Conference on the Socratic Dialogue. Even more participants this time, not only from different countries in Europe but also from different continents. Welcome everybody!

For the conference in Hillcroft College in 1996 the three facilitators, Rene Saran, Pieter Mostert and Dieter Krohn, had agreed on a statement on the Socratic Dialogue that was given to the participants as a kind of introduction to the method. It comprises some fundamental ideas, information about the procedures and the rules for participants and facilitators as well as criteria for suitable examples. This statement may serve here as a first introduction for those who are not so familiar with the Socratic Dialogue and as a starting point for a critical review of the ideas presented:

What is a Socratic Dialogue?

A Socratic dialogue is a joint attempt to find the answer to a fundamental question. The question is the centre of the dialogue. It is applied to a concrete experience of one or more of the participants that is accessible to all other participants. Systematic reflection upon this experience is accompanied by a search for shared judgements and underlying reasons for these.

The dialogue aims at consensus. Whilst it is possible to achieve consensus, this is not a simple or easy task. Effort, discipline and perseverance are required. Everyone's thoughts need to be clarified in such a manner that participants understand each other fully. Explanations and reasons are analysed and weighed-up carefully. The discourse moves slowly and systematically so that all participants gain insight into the substance of the dialogue.

The Socratic dialogue proper is a discourse about *content*, in which the central question is at stake. Heckmann in addition developed the *meta-dialogue* which is about the process and atmosphere of the dialogue. Some facilitators also distinguish a *dialogue about strategy* to determine pathways of the dialogue. Others see strategy questions as an integral part of the Socratic dialogue proper or of the meta-dialogue.

The Socratic dialogue derives its name from Socrates, but it is not an imitation of a Platonic dialogue. What is basically Socratic is the method of rigorous inquiry into the thoughts, concepts and values we hold as true. The Socratic dialogue is a joint investigation into assumptions we make when we formulate our thoughts.

Procedures

The Socratic dialogue normally uses the following procedures:

(1) A well-formulated, general question, or a statement, is set by the facilitator before the discourse commences.
(2) The first step is to collect concrete examples experienced by participants in which the given topic plays a key role.
(3) One example is chosen by the group which will usually be the basis of the analysis and argumentation throughout the dialogue.
(4) Crucial statements made by participants are written down on a flip chart or board, so that all can have an overview and be clear about the sequence of the discourse.

Rules for Participants

There a seven basic rules for participants in the Socratic dialogue:

(1) Each participant's contribution is based upon what s/he has experienced, not upon what s/he has read or heard.
(2) The thinking and questioning is honest. This means that only genuine doubts about what has been said should be expressed.
(3) It is the responsibility of all participants to express their thoughts as clearly and concisely as possible, so that everyone is able to build on the ideas contributed by others earlier in the dialogue.
(4) Participants should not concentrate exclusively on their own thoughts, they should make every effort to understand those of other participants and if necessary seek clarification.
(5) Anyone who has lost sight of the question or of the thread of the discussion should seek the help of others to clarify where the group stands.
(6) Abstract statements should be grounded in concrete experience in order to illuminate such statements.
(7) Inquiry into relevant questions continues as long as participants either hold conflicting views or have not yet reached clarity.

Rules for Facilitators

(1) The main task of the facilitator is to assist the joint process of clarification so that any achieved consensus is genuine. Consensus is only achieved when contradictory points of view have been resolved and all arguments and counter-arguments have been fully considered; the facilitator has to ensure this happens.

(2) The facilitator should not 'steer' the discussion in one particular direction nor take a position in matters of content; s/he should ensure that the rules of the dialogue are upheld.

Criteria for suitable examples

(1) The example has been derived from the participant's own experience; hypothetical or 'generalized' examples ['quite often it happens to me that ...'] are not suitable.

(2) Examples should not be very complicated ones; simple ones are often the best. Where a sequence of events has been presented, it would be best for the group to concentrate on *one* aspect or *one* event.

(3) The example has to be relevant for the topic of the dialogue and of interest to the other participants. Furthermore, all participants must be able to put themselves into the shoes of the person giving the example.

(4) The example should deal with an experience that has already come to an end. If the participant is still immersed in the experience it is not suitable. For example, if decisions are still to be taken, there is a risk that group members might be judgmental or spin hypothetical thoughts.

(5) The participant giving the example has to be willing to present it fully and provide all the relevant factual information and answer questions so that the other participants are able to understand the example and its relevance to the central question.

Loccum 2000

We can use this statement above as a point of reference or as a stumbling block. This conference in Loccum gives us the chance:

- to share our experience in the Socratic Dialogue,
- to sharpen our awareness of details,
- to review theoretical assumptions,
- to put old believes to the test,
- to develop new ideas,
- to promote understanding and cooperation among the "Socratics",
- to enjoy the week and
- to have fun together.

Last but not least: Thanks to the planning group: Rene Saran for the Society for the Furtherance of Critical Philosophy; Dries Boele, Erik Boers, Hans Bolten, Jos Kessels and Pieter Mostert alternately for the Dutch Socratics; Horst Gronke, Dieter Krohn, Rainer Loska, Kirsten Malmquist, Klaus Roß, and Nora Walter for the Philosophisch-Politische Akademie and the Gesellschaft für Sokratisches Philosophieren respectively.

And many, many thanks to Peter Brune and Uwe Nitsch for their masterpiece of organization so far. Let us hope and make sure that things go smoothly.

Lectures

Erik Boers

On Our Duty to Use the Socratic Dialogue in Business Organizations[1]

1. Introduction

Within the community of people working with Socratic Dialogues, following the traditon set by Nelson and Heckmann, there are some major concerns about the use of this method within the context of business organizations:

a) Some fear that the method might be used as an instrument for secondary purposes, like problem-solving or manipulating employees, instead of searching for the truth.

b) Consultants offering Socratic Dialogues professionally, could be tempted to please the client by reducing the extent of fundamental critical thinking.

c) Time pressure sometimes requires that Socratic Dialogues in organizations be shortened. This raises the question whether these conversations still deserve the predicate 'Socratic Dialogue'. Should we then not reserve this predicate for sessions held in a more contemplative setting?

We talked about these concerns during the *International Conference on Socratic Dialogue and Ethics*, July 2000 in Loccum (Germany). This article is an elaboration of the short improvised talk I held there. Referring to the title of this conference my proposition is:

'Ethics' requires us to extend conducting Socratic Dialogues from the customary contexts to business organizations and to adjust the method to these specific circumstances.

---

1   In the title I refer to business organizations, but everything I write can also be applied to governmental and other 'not-for-profit' organizations.

2. Philosophy as a way of life

I am a philosopher, which means that for me it is not satisfying to live my life without examining it. To inform this examination I chose to acquaint myself with and follow the tradition of Western Philosophy and I stand in a tradition founded by thinkers like Socrates, Epictetus, Anselm, Hume, Kant, Nietzsche, Wittgenstein, Popper, Levinas, Nelson and Heckmann. I have been inspired by their writings and by the records of their lives. To them and to the people I work and live with I try to account for my own thinking and acting.

These philosophers saw philosophy as a way of life. As an illustration I would like to quote Epictetus, a famous Stoic philosopher from the first century.

> "Philosophy comes down, in the first place and inevitably, to the application of fundamental moral theorems, such as, "We ought not to lie". In the second place philosophy concerns itself with proof, or demonstration, for example "Why is lying wrong?" And finally philosophy concerns itself with the foundations, the fundamental analysis: "What makes this a proof? What is demonstration? What is a conclusion? What is contradiction? What is true and what is false?"
>
> The third topic, then, is essential for the second, and the second for the first, which cannot be circumvented and which requires quiet deliberation and discussion. But we usually turn matters around. We spend all our time and focus all our attention on the third topic and neglect entirely the first. As a consequence we lie, and simultaneously have an abundance of arguments at our disposal to explain why lying is wrong." (Epitectus, Encheiridion, 51)

For me this quotation means that we philosophize in order to live a good life, or rather, to establish a good life for all. Epictetus makes clear that philosophy is a practice 'using moral theorems'. The proof of our understanding is to be found in our acts. True understanding leads to right behaviour. If we fail to act in accordance with our comprehension, we do not really know the truth. And it is from our own acts that we can learn the truths we cherish.

3. The misleading distinction between 'search for ttruth' and 'practical application'

In my first lines I paraphrased Socrates' motto 'an unexamined life is not worth living'. The counterpart is 'it is useless to examine our lives without checking our knowledge by trying to live according to our conclusions'. Truth cannot be sought other than within a practical context. The proposed distinction between the Socratic Method as a search for truth and the practical application of this method in the business environment is illusory. There always has been a practical context in which the Socratic Method was employed: the educational context, the political context or the environment of everyday life. We have become used to identify the method with these contexts and with the routines which fit there best. But we should not limit the method to these contexts and routines. The method can be used in many contexts. The business organization is one of them, and a very important one.

4. Our lives in organizations

As a follower of the Western philosophical tradition I am inclined to practice philosophy in the context of everyday life. After all, where else is the good life to be found? Nowadays we live in an age dominated by organizations. People spend most of their time, attention, energy and creativity in their organizational lives. Occupation and profession largely determine our identity. Our lives and our views about the 'good life' are dominated by organizations. That is why we must philosophize with employers, employees and managers: we want to learn about the good life from their experience and we want them to examine critically their ways of living and working together.

For this reason I have chosen to work as a philosopher-consultant in organizations, both profit and non-profit. Eleven years of management consulting have taught me to see organizations primarily as learning environments for all concerned. Having finished their formal education employees start to define their professional goals and style while learning to take into account the interests of their colleagues and competitors.

Later on in their careers they might choose to supervise or provide leadership to their colleagues. They then need to explore, for example, the boundaries of their responsibilities and the meaningfulness of the formulated collective ambition.

In these different phases of personal and professional development all kinds of fundamental questions arise; questions concerning integrity, responsibility, flexibility, success, motivation, effectiveness, mutuality, leadership, empowerment, openness, autonomy and so on. And that is where my work as a philosopher-consultant starts.

5. The Socratic Method and our duty as philosophers

Since my first encounter with it some ten years ago I have learned to value the Socratic Method, based on the critical philosophy developed by Leonard Nelson and Gustav Heckman, as a genuine and fertile way of philosophizing in everyday life. It encourages participants to take responsibility for their own thinking and at the same time stimulates them to think together. There is a profound question (touching the cornerstones of our lives) at stake, which always gets connected to participants' personal experience. The method constitutes an ethical practice: we think about philosophical issues and try to behave in accordance with the way we think together.

The method is extremely suitable for the questions referred to at the end of the preceding section. The questions are fundamental and closely related to issues of everyday life. The people involved need not only to come to grips with these questions, but they are also forced to practice the insights gained during the inquiry and learn from them. If these people ask for guidance, we as philosophers have the obligation to offer our experience. If we do not answer their call, they will be at the mercy of dogmatic management gurus. These sophists of our age all have the tendency to transform any sincere question to their universal answer. Any attempt to think critically for oneself is suffocated in a cloud of success stories.

But there is more at stake. We as philosophers, searching for the good life, can learn a lot about the practical wisdom developed by managers and employees. If these people invite us to talk and think with them, we should seize the opportunity to learn from their experiences in dealing with all kinds of dilemmas while working and living together in organizations.

6. Instrumentalism and outdated views on organizations

Leonard Nelson not only developed a philosophical method but he also founded a political, social democratic movement, called the Internationale Sozialistischer Kampf-Bund. Many of its members lost their lives resisting the Nazi regime. I have not studied this honourable part of political history, but I imagine that the hesitation to be hired by business organizations can be related to this particular aspect of the background of the Nelsonian tradition, which is still shared by many Socratics. Their warnings (instrumentalization in order to manipulate people; corruption of the method by commercial interests) seem to be inspired by a specific perception of the concepts of 'instrument' and 'business organizations'.

To address the first: is it wrong to see and use the Socratic Dialogue as an instrument? I do not think so. It is one of the instruments — in addition to reading, writing, contemplating or debating — a philosopher has. Can it be used to manipulate people for one's own benefit? I do not believe that is easily done if we stick to the rules and guidelines which have been handed down for participants. Besides, the way we use the Socratic Method in business organizations helps and indeed forces people to clarify their own aims and goals (their true interests). But are employees really free to think critically about these? I would certainly think so. We are living in an information society. Most of the employees and managers I meet are knowledge workers with professional responsibility for determining their own objectives and the methods they employ. They are asked to think critically about the foundations of their profession, though they have rarely been educated to do so. If we take a close look at the world of business organizations, we see that compared with the first half of the 20th Century it has changed dramatically. Classical distinctions between owner and employee, labour and control, structure and strategy, inside and outside, profit and non-profit, private and public, competitor and partner, customer and supplier have become blurred. To obtain a clear view on the need for dialogue and the possibilities for the Socratic Method in business organizations, we have to shake off our 19th century ideas about privately owned companies and the subordinate role of employees. The roles of organizations have changed and it is unwise to stick to the initial choice of developing the Socratic Method merely in educational and political organizations.

In principle, therefore, it is both possible and advisable to conduct a Socratic Dialogue in business organizations. In practice, of course, all kinds of tensions appear. People working together in organizations, including consultants, inevitably develop all kinds of interdependencies. There are many interests at stake. Do these make us less free as facilitators and participants? I do not think so. Our freedom depends on the way we deal with our own interests (as facilitator, as client or as participant). If we let them dominate us and use the Socratic Dialogue, for example, for 'problem solving', 'conflict mediation' or 'policy making' than we are misusing the method. But if we acknowledge our interests and create some distance towards them, we can conduct a genuine inquiry.

7.   The necessity to adjust the method

It is not easy to conduct a Socratic Dialogue. It is undoubtedly more difficult to do so in an organizational setting. People in business organizations, like others, are simultaneously attracted and deterred by the precision and slow pace of the Socratic Dialogue. As facilitators we have the responsibility to find ways of helping them to endure this ambiguity.

In order to succeed we need to make some adjustments. I still use the traditional procedure (question — example selection — enquiry in basic assumptions) and the traditional rules for participants. But I work with different kinds of groups, e.g. management teams (after a merger, thinking about common values) or groups of professional colleagues (examining the core of their profession). The number of participants varies from 4 to 30 people. And the duration of the sessions varies a great deal: sometimes I conduct a Socratic Dialogue in one day or in a sequence of two-hour sessions with homework in between or in a two-day session alternated with dedicated exercises to improve the dialogical skills or even in a session of three hours with a lot of preparation in advance. It even occurs that I facilitate a dialogue together with a Socratic colleague, one of us writing, the other conducting the dialogue, every now and then interviewing each other about the progress.

These are clear deviations from the usual format: groups of 4 to 12 people, one facilitator, duration of 20 hours in the course of a week or a long weekend. But these are not the first adjustments in the Nelsonian tradition. Let me give two examples.

a) Nelson and Heckmann themselves started their dialogues in an educational, classroom setting. It was only later on that the week-long or long-weekend versions appeared.

b) The rather authoritarian way Nelson conducted his Socratic Dialogues at the beginning of the twentieth century is nearly impossible nowadays. Because of the changing relation between teacher and student, around 1965 Heckman and others introduced the meta-dialogue as a crucial element of the method. Participants wanted to deal openly with their feelings of (dis)comfort and they were not willing to follow a method without proper understanding.

These examples demonstrate that the adaptation of the method to changing circumstances is not only necessary, but that it is common practice in the Nelsonian tradition.

8. The inappropriateness of protecting the method

Of course we will want to assess whether the variations we develop in business organizations still meet the criteria for a Socratic Dialogue. That is no easy matter. In order to protect the essence we find ourselves inclined to define a standard practice, generate formal criteria, design compulsory courses, entitle certain practices to carry the predicate 'Socratic Dialogue' and even register this name officially. But as I have stated before: there is no standard practice of the Socratic Method. There is only a standard or preferred context (educational or political). And even in this standard context, every facilitator has his or her own style which has a great impact on the proceedings and on the result. Participants do not choose only for the method but also for the person who conducts the dialogue. In the way in which the facilitator works they experience the integrity and sincerity of his/her philosophy. Moreover, my life as a consultant and management trainer has taught me that it is impossible to protect a method from improper use. Anyone who gets excited about it will be inclined to experiment with it. There is no (legal) way you can stop them.

There is no standard practice and there is no way to legally protect a method (or parts of it). I even think that it is not desirable to protect the Socratic Method by standardization and registration. I consider every Socratic Dialogue as a worthwhile attempt to philosophize. We can learn from the failures and successes of ourselves and of others. To keep our ideals alive, the method should not be fenced in. It needs to be fed by new experiences. Instead of excluding people who experiment on their own behalf, we should form a community to exchange experiences, work together and account for our attempts. The Socratic Method is not to be treated like a patented product or a registered trademark. We would do better to think of it as a living tradition, handed down from one person to another, with no clear boundaries but with a recognizable practice and a common language. This shows us the way to keep our tradition alive: organize a community of practitioners to share experience, develop a common language, maintain rules of conduct and initiate newcomers. [2]

References

Conference folder (July 2000): Socratic Dialogue and Ethics.
Epictetus (1996): Encheiridion. Edited by James Frieser, Internet Release.
Hadot, P. (1995): Philosophy as a Way of Life. Oxford: Blackwell.
Huczynski, A. (1992): Management Gurus and the 12 Secrets of their Success. In: Leadership and Organization Development. Vol. 13, no. 5.

---

2 I wish to thank Edgar Karssing who encouraged me to write this article, my colleagues Pieter Mostert, Jos Kessels, and Piet Breed who commented critically on the first draft and Nico Swaan for polishing my English.

McCloskey, D. N.; Klamer, A. (1995): One Quarter of GDP is Persuasion. In: American Economic Review, May.

Morris, T. (1997): If Aristotle Ran General Motors. New York: H. Holt & Comp.

Nussbaum, M. C. (1994): The Therapy of Desire. New Jersey: Princeton University Press.

Toulmin, S. (1990): Cosmopolis: The Hidden Agenda of Modernity. New York: The Free Press.

Horst Gronke

Socratic Dialogue or Para-Socratic Dialogue?

Socratic-Oriented Dialogue as the Third Way of a Responsible Consulting and Counselling Practice

"One who advises a sick man, living in a way to injure his health, must first effect a reform in his way of living, must he not? And if the patient consents to such a reform, then he may admonish him on other points? If, however, the patient refuses, in my opinion it would be the act of a real man and a good physician to keep clear of advising such a man — the act of a poltroon and a quack on the other hand to advise him further on those terms. The same thing holds in the case of a city, whether it have one master or many.

If a government that proceeds in orderly fashion along the right course, seeks advice about its advantage in some matter, it would be the act of an intelligent man to give advice to such a community. In the case, however, of those who are altogether astray from the path of right government, and will by no means consent to go on the track of it, who on the other hand give notice to their adviser to keep his hands off the constitution under penalty of death if he disobeys, and order him to cater to their wishes and desires by pointing out the easiest and quickest method of attaining them permanently, in that case I should think the adviser who consented to such conditions a poltroon — the one who refused, a real man." (Plato, Letter VII, 330c-331a)

In the following I will discuss the question of how it is possible for consultants and counsellors to carry out Socratic dialogues in 'outside organizations' (organizations in the practical world *outside* of the pure theoretical world) in a responsible manner. First, I will say a few words about Socratic Dialogue and its use in general (1). Then, I will try to give a definition of Socratic Dialogue (2). After that, I will describe ethical problems which are likely to arise if a Socratic Dialogue is carried out in an outside organization (3). Finally, I will turn to my main point which is to outline an ethical theory of a responsible use of Socratic Dialogue (4).

1. The use of Socratic Dialogue

In an abbreviated way of speaking we can say: Socratic Dialogue is not only a method but also an attitude — and a principle.

As a *method* (i.e. starting with a general question and an example, proceeding step by step, writing on a flipchart etc.) Socratic Dialogue can be used for different purposes — ethically good or bad purposes.

As an *attitude* Socratic Dialogue is grounded in values and value-based virtues (tolerance, patience, discipline, integrity, responsibility, sincerity, solidarity etc.) judged by most of us as ethically good. But these values and virtues are not necessarily and not in all circumstances good values and virtues.

As a *principle* Socratic Dialogue is grounded in reason. That means Socratic Dialogue is the medium of reason in which reason recognises itself and the principle of reason.

Socrates was the first philosopher who discovered and formulated such a principle, the so-called *logos-principle,* in the dialogue with his friend and pupil Kriton who advised him to escape from the death penalty:

> "You know that this is not a new idea of mine; it has always been my nature never to accept advice from any of my friends unless reflection shows that it is the best course that reason offers." (Platon, Kriton, 46b)

It is not tradition, not common sense, not authority, not feeling, not religion, not God, not institutions, not established values, not the majority view, not the ideal personality (vir bonus, spoudaios, phronimos), not the inner perception of a wise person or the inner voice that have the right to decide about truth and justice. All of them are objects of reasonable critique, of critical examination at 'the court of reason' (Kant).[1]

Socratic Dialogue (SD), as established by the German philosophers Leonard Nelson and Gustav Heckmann, is part of the post-Kantian movement of the *'Critical Philosophy'* (CP). Therefore, this kind of *Socratic Dialogue*[CP] is not introduced primarily as a pragmatic means to help people and organizations to reach their several aims (i.e. success, happiness, self-confidence, good teamwork etc.). Originally, a Socratic

---

1   This makes the difference of the Platonic to the Aristotelian and Ciceronian tradition.

Dialogue[CP] was not a dialogue offered by consultants and counsellors. Socrates, Nelson and Heckmann were not consultants and counsellors. On the contrary, the Socratic Dialogue[CP] is introduced by them to clarify people's claims in matters of truth and justice in a radically critical manner. Originally, a Socratic Dialogue[CP] was a 'court of reason'. Socrates, Nelson and Heckmann were reasonable critics.

Nevertheless it is a fact that today Socratic Dialogues are offered 'outside', to people and organizations as a means to overcome their difficulties in reaching their aims. And we can see that at least sometimes this succeeds. It's obvious that a Socratic 'think audit' can influence personal and organizational practice in a good way. Socratic Dialogue has become a new product on the consulting market and the demand for this product is increasing little by little.

Under these circumstances it is understandable that some philosophers, and other intellectuals who work as freelancers or are out of work, try to earn their living by offering this philosophically grounded product to firms and organizations. The intention of earning money they and some of us have is not bad in itself but can be a source of the misuse of Socratic Dialogue, especially if it leads to the original intention of Socratic Dialogue, critical thinking, being pushed back or even destroyed. In short: Socrates may *go on* the market, but he must *not become part of* the market.

The question I try to answer now is: under which circumstances is using a Socratic Dialogue in the wider society, especially in the administration and business world, ethically responsible? I think the answer to this question will help the Socratic consultants and counsellors to get a clearer idea of their ethical room for manoeuvre and give them greater confidence to act. Socratic facilitators with high claims to quality must be willing to inquire into and legitimate their own practice; otherwise they cannot convincingly offer a concept of consulting which calls for self-inquiry on the part of the managers and staff of an organization.

To identify the ethical problems Socratic Dialogue may raise I start with a short definition and an overview of the essential elements of the Socratic Dialogue[CP].

2. Definition of Socratic Dialogue[CP]

In a Socratic Dialogue[CP] a group of dialogue partners try to answer a Socratic Question (SQ) in a Socratic Manner (SM).

$$SQ + SM = SD^{CP}$$

A Socratic question is a philosophical question (or a question which can easily be transformed into a philosophical question) which is so general and fundamental that it can almost exclusively be answered — in the frame of common experience — by pure thinking. Socratic questions are questions like 'What is truth?' 'Are there universal human rights?' 'What are we responsible for?' Socratic questions are neither questions the answering of which needs empirical knowledge nor questions that are related to concrete situations. They are neither so-called 'How' questions like 'How to improve teamwork?' 'How to persuade people?' 'How to reach happiness?' nor situation-related questions like 'Shall I study philosophy or science?' 'Was the Kosovo intervention of NATO responsible or not?' 'Should Great Britain join the European union or not?'[2]

A Socratic manner is a particular form of dialogical argumentation between at least two dialogue partners in which all of them, with the help of a Socratic facilitator, try to find the best possible knowledge about the true answer (truth) to a Socratic question.

In my opinion there are *four essential elements* of such a Socratic Dialogue:

- First, a dialogue conducted in a Socratic manner *is primarily oriented in the finding of truth*, not in self-experience, not in good interpersonal relations, nor in intellectual amusement.
- Second, thinking Socratically means *to think concretely*. All remarks should be related to real experience. Otherwise the dialogue could raise a lot of meaningless speculation.
- Third, a participant in a Socratic Dialogue should only accept the argument which — as Socrates said — 'appears to him to be the best' (Platon, Kriton, 46 b). *Thinking for yourself* means to raise your

---

2 Though the preceding discussion of a Socratic question can *help* answering empirical and situation-related questions in a more reasonable and more sustainable manner.

own questions, doubts and arguments and to trust in your own ability to obtain reasonable insight.

- Fourth, a Socratic group is a group of common thinkers where each has confidence in the ability of their dialogue partners to find the truth. Therefore they are interested in mutual understanding and mutual agreement to a presented statement. To seek the truth means *to try to reach a reasonable consensus* between the group participants.

3. Ethical problems which are likely to arise if a Socratic Dialogue is carried out in an outside organization

On the basis of this definition of a Socratic Dialogue[CP] we can list possible ways in which ethical misuse of the Socratic method might occur. In this I distinguish between a misuse of the Socratic method that is obviously ethically irresponsible and a misuse that could be but is not necessarily ethically irresponsible, it may even be ethically responsible.

In any case irresponsibility is for example:

- offering a Socratic Dialogue for problems which cannot be solved by a Socratic dialogue;
- instrumentalising a Socratic Dialogue for an obviously ethically problematic purpose (i.e. improving the teamwork of a group of racists);
- posing a Socratic question (SQ) which embraces an ethically problematic purpose (i.e. how can I manipulate people?);
- offering a Socratic Dialogue as an unqualified Socratic facilitator;
- pushing desired results, blocking undesired results;
- siding with some participants, supporting hierarchy;
- playing with people's emotions, offending participants;
- betrayal of trust (i.e. passing on information about participants);
- intentional misrepresentation of the results of the dialogue in the report.

To prevent such kinds of misuse we need:

(1) a clear definition of what a Socratic Dialogue[CP] is;
(2) national and international agreements of qualified Socratic facilitators about ethical codes of Socratic facilitating — and *maybe (if possible)*
(3) protection of Socratic Dialogue[CP] by patent.

But more interesting for my purpose is that use of Socratic Dialogue which seems to be but is not necessarily and not in all respects ethically irresponsible, for example:

- giving wrong or incomplete information on the potential consequences of a Socratic Dialogue;
- excluding people who are concerned with the decisions that are to be influenced by the Socratic Dialogue;
- guiding instead of facilitating;
- pushing or blocking particular methods of argumentation;
- offering a dialogue which is not to all intents and purposes a Socratic Dialogue as a Socratic Dialogue.

Let us see why this kind of misuse of the Socratic Dialogue[CP] seems at first sight to be irresponsible. What does it imply to offer a Socratic Dialogue to outside organizations which employ Socratic facilitators as paid outside consultants in order to help solve a pragmatic problem in these organizations?

I think it implies at least that one has to *present the Socratic Dialogue as an instrument*, namely as an instrument that can be utilised for a change of consciousness and attitude, which could be of use for the various purposes of the customer.

The Socratic consultants who want to sell their product say things — must say things — like 'Socratic Dialogue trains teamwork, that's good for the work of project teams', 'Socratic Dialogue improves mutual understanding, that's good for knowledge and information transfer in your organization', 'Socratic Dialogue helps clarify the value attitudes of the staff, that's good for their motivation and involvement', etc. In short, to sell their product the Socratic consultants must emphasise its instrumental character. In my opinion these sentences are not false. In most cases such consequences do occur. And probably Socratic Dialogue is the best method to fulfil these kinds of aims in organizations which do not strongly reflect psychodynamic and hierarchic problems and have reached a sufficient level of reasonable behaviour among the staff.

But because Socratic Dialogue^{CP} is *originally and essentially not an instrument*, the Socratic consultants tend to hide the main aspect of the Socratic dialogue, namely its critical aspect. That can lead to behaviour like the following:

- not telling the customer of the possibility that it is not merely his situation-related aims and values that will be criticised, but also his fundamental aims and values;
- formulating a starting question the structure of which prevents critique of the fundamental orientation of an organization;
- excluding elements (i.e. a group of staff, types of examples) which could raise fundamental critical questions;
- conducting the dialogue in such a way that fundamental critical questions cannot arise;
- blocking critical results which are not 'savoury' for the customer.

These are some ethically problematic kinds of Socratic consulting practice. *But are they ethically irresponsible?* I would say: yes and no. It depends. It depends on the circumstances of the situation.

Here we have a typical problem of the ethics of responsibility, a conflict between idealistic and pragmatic orientations. At first sight this problem seems to lead to a Socratic aporia: On the one hand we feel the duty to support the efforts at cultivating the fundamental critical thinking in more or less ideal Socratic Dialogues (corresponding to the Socratic logos principle), on the other hand we must accept that establishing Socratic Dialogues in the world of practical life implies a pragmatic reduction of fundamental critical thinking.

In the last few years I have experienced some fruitless discussions about this conflict. Some discussions among the Socratic facilitators were characterised either by an antagonistic dispute of contrary positions or a denial and diminution of this problem. Therefore I have thought and am still thinking about a constructive concept which takes both sides into account: a third way between pragmatism and idealism for the Socratic consulting practice.

4. Ethical theory of a responsible use of Socratic Dialogue

Let me outline these first steps of this concept in some short remarks. The fundamental idea is that both the idealistic way and the pragmatic way of conducting an Outside Socratic Dialogue can be either responsible or irresponsible.

The idealistic way is responsible if the conditions of the situation are nearly ideal, if the situation is not strongly burdened by the pressure of action and decision. I think realising what I call Inside Socratic Dialogues[3], namely dialogues organized inside the universe of discourse and not outside, in the world of practice, is a serious task. For children and adults need such Inside Socratic Dialogues and a 'holiday'-like space for them (i.e. like the Socratic weeks or weekends offered by the GSP) to learn deep critical thinking. Inside Socratic Dialogues can influence people's general way of thinking and living in the long run.

On the other hand, Inside Socratic Dialogues can rarely influence people's individual actions and decisions directly. They are not immediately helpful in the outside world where time is money, where people have no time to discuss problems in extenso. Here people have to decide within a limited time or space, in a competitive, even antagonistic society in which moral awareness is not in great prominence and moral or dialogical behaviour is often not to be expected. That means in many cases, i.e. in the case of pragmatic problems in a business organization, it is irresponsible to offer an Inside Socratic Dialogue for the solution of concrete practical problems. It is irresponsible because the consequences of an individual dialogical behaviour in the world of practical life are possibly not tolerable; consequences like disadvantage, fiasco, bankruptcy, dismissal, or poverty.

Nevertheless, I think it is equally wrong to conduct an Outside Socratic Dialogue in that pragmatic way which implies a secret instrumentalisation of the Socratic Dialogue for the purposes of the real-life world. That pragmatic instrumentalisation means in most cases to

---

3 'Inside' and 'outside' is a classical distinction in philosophy. In the history of Western and Eastern philosophy people have often thought that truth can be found if the influence from the outside world is excluded. Most of today's philosophers don't think that such an exclusion is completely possible.

offer a dialogue as a Socratic Dialogue[CP] although it is not Socratic in a full sense because it is missing some essential elements of a Socratic Dialogue[CP].

For example, we know by experience that a so-called short-term dialogue of three or six hours or a pro- and contra-discourse of a similar space of time conducted under the conditions of success in the business world cannot include all four essential elements of a Socratic Dialogue[CP]. In many cases one or two of these elements, mostly the elements of thinking for yourself and thinking together, are reduced. Although the structure of these dialogues is in some respects *similar* to the structure of a SD[CP] they are not Socratic Dialogues[CP]. Therefore it is irresponsible to promise a Socratic Dialogue[CP] (a dialogue of critical thinking) in these cases.[4]

But this judgement does not imply that offering an imperfect Socratic Dialogue[CP] is necessarily irresponsible. If the Socratic Dialogue[CP] is a valuable method to improve our critical thinking in several topic areas (epistemology, ethics, aesthetics) we are well-advised to introduce as much of it as possible into the world of practical life. It is better and more responsible to offer an imperfect Socratic Dialogue than no Socratic Dialogue.

Even the late Plato recognised that in the field of political affairs acting like a 'moderate' idealist or a 'gentleman' (acting in correspondence to one's pure ethical conviction) as well as acting like a radically 'courageous' pragmatist (acting in a mainly success-oriented way) would be irresponsible. The philosopher advised the politicians who are responsible for the organization of the conditions of public life to look for the most reasonable mixture of the moderate and the courageous character, let us say: to look for the golden mean between idealism and pragmatism.

"Because if a courageous character is reproduced for many generations without any admixture of the moderate type, the natural course of development is that at first it becomes superlatively powerful but in the

---

4   To avoid misunderstandings: I do not think that short-term dialogues and dilemma trainings or 'mixed' dialogues are immoral or that their application to the outside world of practice is principally irresponsible. I use these procedures in my own teaching and consulting practice. The question is: under which circumstances is the use of these procedures legitimate?

end it breaks out into sheer fury and madness. [...] But the character which is too full of modest reticence and untinged by valor and audacity, if reproduced after its kind for many generations, becomes too dull to respond to the challenges of life and in the end becomes quite incapable of acting at all. [...] Magistrates of the moderate type are exceedingly cautious, fair, and tenacious of precedent, but they lack pungency and the drive which makes for efficiency. [...] The courageous type for their part have far less of the gifts of fairness than their moderate brethren, but they have in a marked degree the drive that gets things done. A community can never function well either in the personal intercourse of its citizens or in its public activities unless both of these elements of character are present and active. [...] Now we have reached the appointed end of the weaving of the web of state. It is fashioned by the Statesman's weaving; the strands run true, and these strands are the gentle and the brave. Here these strands are woven together into a unified character. For this unity is won where the kingly art draws the life of both types into a true fellowship by mutual concord and by ties of friendship. It is the finest and best of all fabrics. It enfolds all who dwell in the city, bond or free, in its firm contexture. Its kingly weaver maintains his control and oversight over it, and it lacks nothing that makes for happiness so far as happiness is obtainable in a human community." (Plato, Statesman, 311b-c)

My proposal for a responsible way to conduct a Socratic consulting practice is to develop a theory of *Socratic-Oriented Dialogues*. It seems to me that a responsible Socratic *consulting* and *counselling* practice is a practice of *Socratic-Oriented Dialogues*.

As a first step to develop such a theory I propose to distinguish the use of the concept of Socratic Dialogue in a broader sense and in a strict sense. The concept of Socratic Dialogue used in a broader sense implicates both Socratic Dialogues of a strict sense, Socratic Dialogues[CP], and Socratic-Oriented Dialogues.[5] Those dialogues which are offered as, but are not, really Socratic Dialogues, even not Socratic-Oriented Dialogues, I propose to call *Para-Socratic Dialogues*.[6] In this way we are getting the following classification:

---

5 That is not a problem of name-giving but of characterization and of differentiation.

6 Especially facilitators without a sound practical Socratic education, and also practically qualified Socratic facilors without a good theoretical knowledge of the philosophical roots of the Socratic dialogue, sometimes offer dialogues as Socratic Dialogues which are not Socratic Dialogues but Para-Socratic dialogues.

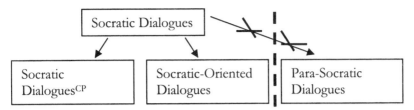

To come to the end I am going to look for some criteria to define the concept of *Socratic-Oriented Dialogue*.

- I think one essential material criterion is that the dialogue is more or less *philosophically-oriented*, that means it is not primarily oriented in the solution of a concrete problem but in the inquiry into the presuppositions that are necessarily required for a reasonable solution of concrete problems.

- Another material criterion is the *content-orientation* of the dialogue, which means, for example, the dialogue is not psychologically-dominated.

- A third material criterion is the *truth-orientation* of the dialogue, which means it must be mainly an exchange of arguments instead of telling stories and so on ...

But material criteria of such a kind will not do. Material criteria are too inflexible, too rigid to guarantee a classification of Socratic-Oriented Dialogues adequate to special conditions. For example, under some conditions it can be very supportive for the process of content-oriented dialogues when — now and then — psychologically-dominated phases of dialogue or even strategic ways of behaviour are inserted. Therefore I think we also need a guideline, a regulative procedural ethical imperative to distinguish flexibly between a Socratic-Oriented Dialogue and a Para-Socratic Dialogue. I suggest the following relatively formal principle here formulated as a rule of thumb:

When, as a Socratic consultant or counsellor, you offer a Socratic-Oriented Dialogue to an outside organization then as much as possible try to realise it in the form of a Socratic Dialogue[CP] (corresponding to the communicative level that the circumstances make possible) and try to reduce as little as feasible the Socratic character of the dialogue (corresponding to the communicative level that the circumstances demand).

That implies among other things the duty to ask yourself seriously: 'How much of a Socratic Dialogue[CP], how much of the essential elements of a Socratic Dialogue[7] can I responsibly realise in such a situation — relating to the consequences of my practice for the stakeholders?' 'What is the range of communication in this situation I have to take into account?' 'Did I close the door to unrestrained critical thinking too early?' etc.

To give reflections of such a kind a frame we are supposed to define the lowest and the highest communicative level for a Socratic-Oriented Dialogue and to define some sub-levels of communication conditions for different kinds of Socratic-Oriented Dialogues.

I think it is necessary to develop such a theory in future. That applies, at least, to those Socratic facilitators who go into this field of the outside world where the rules of the market are dominant. I do not agree with those Socratic practitioners who reject theoretical reflections about that topic or consider them as superfluous. Surely, on the one hand a pure ethical theory without practice is fruitless but on the other hand a pure 'Socratic' consulting or counselling practice without an ethical theory will be blind – and such behaviour of Socratic practitioners would, in any case, not be responsible.

References

Hamilton, Edith; Cairn, Huntington (eds.) (1961): The collected dialogues of Plato, including the letters. Bollingen Series LXXI, New Yersey: Princeton University Press.

---

7 These elements are: starting the dialogue with a clear Socratic question, thinking truth-oriented (aiming at consensus), thinking for yourself (autonomy), arguing in relation to experience, trying to get mutual understanding.

Jos Kessels

What Questions would Socrates ask?
On Dialogue and Ethics in Organizations

Summary

If Socrates could have a dialogue with managers and organizational leaders, what would it be about? How would he get them to investigate themselves and inquire into virtue, knowledge, justice and the other themes of his regular repertoire?

Introductory text

Socratic questions often have no ethical relevance. How does Socrates get managers and organizational leaders to investigate themselves and inquire into virtue?

Reading Plato's transcriptions of Socrates' dialogues I get the following picture. Socrates starts a conversation, about the weather, the latest gossips, how things are going or whatever. In this phase Socrates asks questions that are purely informative and relational: he just wants the conversation to get going. Then after a while some topic arises, a problem someone has, a thing on someone's mind. In a dialogue with managers this could be the internal relations in the organisation, the stress it brings, the lack of clarity in who is responsible for what, or a whole lot of other things. Here the questions Socrates asks seem still to be of a purely personal interest. Then Socrates tries to get the topic formulated in one or more central questions. By now it is clear this is not an ordinary conversation anymore, systematic questioning is coming in, and division of roles, but no ethics. Everything Socrates does is framed in the terminology and the conceptual schemes of the people he is interrogating. In business he would talk about strategy, vision, human resource management, scenarios, business ideas and so on. If he couldn't do that, he would lose his partners in the investigation.

Then, once a topic is formulated in a central question, Socrates will inquire into the different positions of experts on this question, i.e. no ethics. After that, he will try to find one or more central propositions and inquire into the presuppositions of this proposition by asking others to put themselves into the shoes of the one who gave the example: the normal stuff of a Socratic Dialogue, but no ethics. Suppose his partners go that far with him into the inquiry, they make their reasoning and views explicit. Then somewhere there comes a point at which Socrates will ask about the good of all that. This is a tricky spot, because he could easily lose his partners in the inquiry here. So he must keep them interested, he must be able to get them to see the relevance of this further step. Therefore he probably will not even couch his questions in ethical terms here. He will talk about visioning as a necessary condition for strategic planning, about human flourishing as a necessary condition for good work, about competencies instead of virtues, about balance instead of justice, about excellence instead of temperance or courage, about realism instead of truth. In other words, he will avoid ethical terms, though his purpose is always the same: inquiring after virtue.

My contention is that in a business environment the Socratic Dialogue may seem to have no ethical relevance. Nevertheless such a dialogue is to be considered as a genuine Socratic Dialogue, because the final aim and focus is always the same: truth, goodness, beauty, or whatever you name it.

Lecturette

The question

The theme of this conference is '*Ethics and Socratic Dialogue*'. What is the *relationship* between these two? Is every Socratic Dialogue essentially about ethics? Or is there no such privileged connection between Socratic Dialogue and ethics? Are perhaps only some Socratic Dialogues about ethics, depending on what we mean by 'Socratic Dialogue' or on the particular way a dialogue is carried out? These and similar questions were discussed during our conference.

I would like to follow the Socratic convention and present first some of my associations with the question, then a short example, a provisional judgment and some of my underlying assumptions.

Associations

We know that Socrates only inquired into *matters of human concern*. As a young man he got disillusioned about the methods and results of scientific inquiry. After that time he was only interested in discussing human affairs. He is said to have brought philosophy down from the heavens to earth, for he shifted the philosophical focus from investigation of external nature to the investigation of man, from the search for causes and beginnings to the search for *reasons and ends* .

We rarely think about ends. Mostly we take the ends for granted and think only about the means to reach them. Doctors think about how to promote health, businessmen about how to earn money. That health or money are valuable aims is tacitly assumed. They are supposed to be obvious conditions of happiness and a good life, and that is what everyone wants.

Socrates asked the question what *happiness and a good life* (eudaimonia) really mean. His answer was that they are only to be found in *virtue* (aretè), 'in wisdom and truth and the perfection of the soul' (*Apology*), in that which makes men good as individuals or as citizens (Xenophon, Memorabilia, 1, i, 11-16; Cornford 1932, pp. 29 ff.).

To achieve this virtue insight is required into the value of the various things we desire: *virtue is knowledge*. Human perfection lies in the knowledge of good and evil. There are three types of good: pleasure, social significance and wisdom. The knowledge that is required is the knowledge of their interdependence and relative proportion. This type of *knowledge cannot be transferred*, you will not know that this or that is right or good until you can see it directly for yourself. As soon as you can see it for yourself, that knowledge will put out of court what you are told that other people believe. 'Knowledge of values is a matter of direct insight, like seeing that the sky is blue, the grass is green.' (Cornford 1932, p.46).

Besides, learning this knowledge is not learning something new but learning something old: *learning is recollection*. We know already what we want to learn, only in an unclear manner.

An example

Now what does this say about the relationship between ethics and Socratic Dialogue? Most of you know that the Socratic convention is to postpone this question until we have found a proper example in which the question is actually at stake. We analyse a question not just theoretically, but only after it has been tightly connected to a fitting example, a real life experience. I would like to give you a short sketch of one example, a dialogue that Erik Boers and I recently directed with politicians, civil servants, public governors, representatives of pressure groups and consultants. I expect the example to be controversial, but also helpful for our discussions here.

You may have heard about the Dutch 'polder model', a joint deliberation of groups that have conflicting interests, like employers and employees, or industry and environmentalist groups. Since the breakthrough of this model in Dutch politics there has been a trend to involve different social groups in the preparation of complex political decisions. This has the advantage both of increasing public support and enhancing the creativity of decision making. However, there is also a possible disadvantage, i.e. that the parties at the negotiation table come to some deal without the participation of the government, the administration or the parliament, that is, the ones that are politically responsible for a decision. But how can they be responsible for a decision if they are not involved in the negotiations? Or sharper: is polder model deliberation compatible with democratic decision making? This was the question to be addressed.

The example was a hot issue in Dutch politics, the 'green polder deliberation' between the national airport Schiphol and several different interest groups, including the environmentalist movement. Both question and example had been thoroughly prepared before the actual dialogue took place. The whole thing lasted only one afternoon. There were about 25 participants, personally invited by the consultancy firm that organised the symposium. We had a set up in which first the question was explained, then the chairman of the polder deliberation process reported the example and added his private judgment. Then we interrogated a group of three politicians, asking them to put themselves into the shoes of the example-giver. Then another group of five came in and in the end the public.

Now I will not go into the details of the content or the process. I will only make some statements about the example, my assumptions and my answer to the initial question.

Statement

First, my contention is that this is a proper example of a Socratic Dialogue, although in many respects it does not fit the standard model of the GSP.

Second, this inquiry is not an ethical inquiry, although there are many ethical aspects involved.

Assumptions

First, this is a proper example of a Socratic Dialogue, because it is *systematic* in the usual Socratic sense (question, example, judgement, assumptions), and it is in Gustav Heckmann's words *a joint attempt to get nearer to the truth in some topic*. That is, we were inquiring into legitimate reasons and ends, into what virtue and the good life actually meant in this example, into the knowledge that is constitutive for virtue, happiness and the good life. We were inquiring into the balancing of different types of good for different groups of people, or in Nelson's terms into what in this case our *true interests* are.

Second, this inquiry is not an ethical inquiry, at least not in the normal sense of the word. We would not have dared to use words like truth, virtue or the good life. Even the word democracy was difficult to digest for some of the participants. Such words are too big, too abstract, too ideological. The type of people that we were working with preferred to talk as pragmatists and problem - solvers, in terms of 'how to' questions: how to get clear which choices have to be made, how to clarify the dilemmas that play a role, how to come to a joint view of what the problem really is, how to enhance the quality of decision making. I suppose they would, upon reflection, acknowledge the relevance of ethical words like the old Socratic ones: virtue, happiness and the good life. But they do not think in these terms. Ethical language is not their normal, everyday language.

So if Socrates wants to talk with them, get them to investigate themselves and inquire into virtue, the first thing he must do is speak their language. To link up with their concerns he will take over their terminology, avoid big words and ask questions that do not seem to have any ethical relevance, even though his final aim and focus is always the same: truth, goodness, virtue, or whatever you name it.

References

Cornford, Frances Macdonald (1932): Before and after Sokrates. Cambridge: University Press.

Fernando Leal

Every Socratic Dialogue is about Ethics

§ 1   I would like to start with a large caveat: *nobody knows exactly what a Socratic Dialogue is.* This may seem to be paradoxical in view of the fact that the rules have been fixed and every participant and facilitator knows and applies them to the best of their abilities. It is, so to speak, a game we ourselves have invented, so how would we not know what it is? Yet the assumption that we know and understand what we ourselves have 'made' (an assumption historically associated with authors like Vico and Hobbes in the seventeenth century) has been proved incorrect by social science again and again. The Socratic Dialogue (SD), like any other social institution, has developed organically from the activities of many people with several agendas over many years (the SD will soon be a century old). As such, the SD has to be approached empirically, if we really want to understand what it is and what it has become. Nobody knows exactly what a commercial enterprise or a research institute or an industrial workshop or a bureaucratic arrangement or a teaching facility or a reading club or a political party or a social movement is; social science is dedicated to answering this sort of question and it is still far from completely successful. By the same token, nobody knows exactly what the SD is. To find out what it is and what it does to people, we need empirical research. I think this viewpoint has at last commanded some degree of acceptance in the SD community and I hope it will command more in the future. So I certainly won't claim to know exactly what a SD is. The present paper is therefore just an attempt to communicate what the SD appears to be from what I have seen and experienced myself in almost 20 years of acquaintance with it — by participating in SDs, facilitating SDs and otherwise observing and reflecting on my experience. I claim no more than that; but also no less.

§ 2   The main argument of this paper runs from § 3 through § 12. The numbering has the purpose of facilitating the discussion. In a nutshell, the argument of §§ 3-12 is: every SD is about ethics no matter what the acknowledged topic might be, *because every SD is about values and there is no way to distinguish between 'ethical' and 'non-ethical' values.* Some reflection on that argument, however, raises further questions which may be of interest, so I added §§ 13-20, which goes into at least a few of those questions. (For this publication I have added some further thoughts reflecting on my experience of the Loccum Conference. See §§ 21-25.)

§ 3   It is accepted practice in the SD community to separate some SDs as 'ethical' from other SDs, labelled 'mathematical' or, more recently, 'epistemological' (and perhaps 'ontological'). Some have even proposed to conduct 'physical' SDs. This classification of SDs may be useful for a variety of purposes, but it also tends to obscure what I think is the common trait of any SD, viz. *that it is essentially concerned with ethics.* This is the thesis I want to present here.

§ 4   My thesis is clearly paradoxical in view of the classification I have just mentioned, which is clearly a classification of topics according to fields of study, either philosophical (ethics, epistemology, metaphysics) or scientific (mathematics, physics). So it seems clear that there are SDs which are presumably 'essentially concerned with ethics' (those would be the 'ethical' ones) and there are SDs which are not so concerned (all the others). To say something different would on the face of it seem to be terribly wrongheaded. And perhaps it is. In the spirit of Socrates, I hope I will be corrected if I am wrong.

§ 5   But hold on! Some people may want to say that perhaps what I mean when I say that an SD is 'essentially concerned with ethics' is simply that an SD should be conducted ethically or that it should make people more ethical. Well, no, that's not what I mean. Of course, I'm all for such worthy goals, but I'm not talking about them here. For here I'm not talking about what the SD *should be,* but only about what it actually *is* (as far as my experience reaches, and keeping an eye on the caveat of § 1). I don't have the slightest idea whether the SD, as a matter of fact, is conducted ethically (always? most of the time?) or whether it does, as a matter of fact, make people more ethical (some more than others?). I hope it is and does. But I don't know; and, as far as I can see, neither does anybody. Nevertheless, I think that all SDs, no matter what the topic may be, are essentially concerned with ethics, or to put it even more clearly: they are *about ethics.*

§ 6   What makes a given topic 'ethical'? Or for that matter: what makes a given topic 'non-ethical'? I imagine the standard answer in the

43

SD community would be to give examples rather than attempt a definition. Everyone will probably accept that topics like justice and injustice, equality and discrimination, fairness and privilege, freedom and oppression, solidarity and enmity, rights and duties, virtues and vices, good and evil, right and wrong, justification and condemnation, are 'ethical'. One can even become more specific and mention topics like courage and cowardice, generosity and meanness, friendliness and cruelty, love and hatred, sympathy and envy, pleasure and pain, etc. And we could even give examples of particular questions, either as starting points of individual dialogues ('Are freedom and equality compatible?') or as elaborations and developments of those in the course of individual dialogues ('Did Peter have good reasons for being afraid of Paul in the example?'). Although it may be difficult to define precisely what an 'ethical' topic is, we seem to be pretty good at recognizing them. And *an 'ethical' topic seems to be miles away from, say, a 'mathematical' topic* (e.g. 'Can we draw a circle around any four points lying on a plane?').

§ 7   Although it seems to be quite difficult to define precisely what an 'ethical' topic is, I think it is not unduly unfair to say that they all have to do with our *values*. Some people find this word ('values') a bit bland or vague, and they would rather say that ethics has to do with *principles*. 'Principles' are apparently more robust and important and definite than 'values'. And although there are reasons why I prefer to talk about values than about principles, the fact of the matter is that those reasons are not important for my present argument. Everything I will be saying about values can also be said about principles.

§ 8   The consequence of all this would appear to be that, when we are conducting an SD about justice or equal treatment or the golden rule we are dealing with values, but when we are conducting an SD about circles and points on a plane or about numbers we are *not* dealing with values. Therefore I would be wrong to say that every SD is about values. Plainly, a mathematical SD is *not* about values. So it is *not* ethical.

§ 9   Such a conclusion confuses *mathematics* (a complex and variegated intellectual discipline) with a *mathematical* SD. I would be prepared to concede that mathematics, as a special field, *is not* about values; and even that ethics, insofar as it is a special field, *is* about values. Thus it makes sense to use values as a criterion to distinguish mathematics and ethics as special fields of study. Yet it does not necessarily make sense to use values as a criterion to distinguish mathematical and ethical SDs.

§ 10   In fact, I think that what is really at stake in a mathematical SD is nothing less than *values*. Which values? The values that make up the mathematician's life, the values associated with the kinds of things (the infinite, the continuum, order, space and number) that a mathematician is deeply involved with, the values which, when honoured and cherished and cultivated and acted upon, lead to mathematical discoveries and mathematical insights about those things whose knowledge a mathematician so much praises and so enthusiastically pursues. Which values are these? Well, a probably incomplete list would certainly contain *clarity* of thought, *precision* of expression, *rigour* of deduction, *elegance* of demonstration, *economy* of proof, *generality* of results. The magnificence of these values is as obvious to mathematicians as it is opaque and foreign to non-mathematicians. Mathematicians make an enormous fuss about those values; and we outsiders have not the faintest idea what all the fuss is about. They live for such values; they couldn't live without them. Such values are what make mathematicians tick — but, sadly or happily, not the rest of humankind, which is at best mystified by so much effort and dedication.

§11   'Fine', you might say, 'but what does all that have to do with a mathematical SD?' My contention is that the whole point of a mathematical SD is to give us non-mathematicians a glimpse of those values. We cannot get more than a glimpse, of course, because we are not mathematicians and do not wish to be. It is an occasion, a rare occasion to get at least an idea of what mathematicians are so crazy about, what breathes life into their souls and hearts. It affords us a view into their innermost sanctum. We may not want to remain in that sanctum; we may even forget all about the details of what we saw when a sudden mathematical insight came upon us in the course of an SD. Perhaps only the feeling, or a faint copy of the feeling of awe, will stay with us; or perhaps not even that. But if we participated in a mathematical SD in the right spirit, then we can say that 'we were there', at least for some privileged moments. And that is what a mathematical SD is really and fully about — not the particular contents of this or that problem, but the spirit of the thing, the values that underlie the whole mathematical enterprise. Such an experience is worthwhile. It teaches us something about what it means to be human in that particular way. It is illuminating and edifying. And I recommend it to all non-mathematicians. You won't learn mathematics that way; but you will see mathematics as a way of life.

§ 12 'Okay', you might say, 'but surely such values are not ethical, are they?' Here is the place where a very curious distinction creeps into the picture, viz. the distinction between 'ethical' and 'non-ethical' values. I want to remind you that, up to now, we have distinguished between 'ethical' and 'non-ethical' *topics*. And we have agreed to say that 'ethical' topics concern values (§ 7). And now it seems that we have to distinguish not between 'ethical' and 'non-ethical' topics, but between 'ethical' and 'non-ethical' *values*. And the only argument I can offer to resist this move is to say that I have long looked for a criterion which would allow me to draw such a distinction, and I have failed thus far to find it. My provisional conclusion is, therefore, that *the realm of ethics has no boundaries.* (Hence, if 'ethics' is duly understood as the whole realm of values, then it becomes clear that in a mathematical SD we are learning as much about ethics as we are in a so-called 'ethical' dialogue.) Of course, I may be wrong, but the only way to show me the error of my ways would be to produce such a criterion. As long as such a criterion is not produced, I would keep thinking that all SDs are about ethics because they are all about values, although *not all SDs are of course about the same values.*

§ 13 One consequence of the point of view I am taking here is that the distinction between an 'ethical' SD and a 'non-ethical' (e.g. a mathematical) SD would collapse. Of course, there may still be good reasons, say of a pragmatic, organisational nature, to keep the distinction alive. But from a deep, philosophical perspective there is no such distinction. Nevertheless, I cannot deny there is an important difference in *the way a mathematical SD is conducted* as opposed to a so-called 'ethical' one. (By the way, I am not talking about 'epistemological', 'metaphysical' or 'physical' SDs because I have not experienced them. I have no reason to suspect that my characterization of SDs as 'essentially concerned with ethics' would be shaken by participating in one of those, but I prefer not to speculate about things of which I have no experience.)

§ 14 So what is that procedural difference between a mathematical and a so-called 'ethical' SD? Well, it can easily be described. In a so-called 'ethical' SD an example is given by one of the participants and subsequently analysed by the group. Such an example contains a description of a real situation in the participant's life which purports to be relevant to the topic at hand. In that situation the participant acted in a particular way (in a few cases the action reported may have been an omission rather than a positive action, but that omission also had consequences for the situation). The analysis of the example involves more or less protracted questioning of the example-giver about the details of her example. The answers given to those questions are supposed to be listened to carefully by all participants and constitute the starting point for all sorts of considerations and new questions, all within the topic at hand as it appears to the participants. As opposed to this, in a mathematical SD a 'task' is more or less clearly given by the facilitator at the beginning of the dialogue and participants actively engage in solving that task, although of course the given task can develop in the course of the dialogue and sometimes take an unexpected shape. So it would appear that a mathematical SD is about a problem (a 'mathematical' one) that has to be solved here and now by all participants whereas the 'ethical' SD is, if anything, about a problem (an 'ethical' one) that was solved in a particular way by the participant in her life.

§ 15 Why this difference? I want to suggest that in a mathematical SD the participants are probing the values of the facilitator (who is the mathematician), whereas in a so-called 'ethical' SD the participants are probing the values of the example-giver. The way to probe the values of the facilitator in a mathematical SD is to try to solve a mathematical problem; it seems to be the only way. As opposed to this, the way to probe the values of an example-giver in a so-called 'ethical' SD is to listen to what she has to say about the problem she had to face in her life and how she tried to solve it; it seems to be the only way.

§ 16 So, is this an absolute difference? Might this be the criterion for which I have been looking, a criterion which would allow us to distinguish between 'ethical' and 'non-ethical' values? No, it isn't. First, although it may seem preposterous to try to solve a real 'ethical' problem hands-on (here and now, in real time, all together as a team), in reality nothing prevents the very same structure and rules of an SD being used to think through a problem which still has to be solved. In fact, that was the foremost use of SD within Nelson's political organisations and I think that this is the most promising use for Dutch-style SDs.

§ 17 Secondly, it would be possible to let a mathematician talk about her solution to a mathematical problem, and that way (under the right conditions) to learn a lot about her values as a mathematician.

Nevertheless, the fact that being a mathematician is such a rare thing, it is best to try one's hand at a mathematical problem if we really want to understand what a mathematical life is. In fact, the same thing applies to so-called 'ethical' problems: it is often very difficult to understand what other people did when we lack the experience of particular 'ethical' problems; and it happens that, when we finally face them ourselves, we suddenly come to understand other people.

§ 18   All in all, we should not underestimate the difference between people with respect to their 'ethical' problems. There are selection processes at work in SD organisation which ensures a certain apparent homogeneity of participants; but if we care to listen carefully we will find all sorts of smaller and bigger differences in outlook and values which are not altogether dissimilar to the differences between a mathematician and a non-mathematician. We have some evidence as to those differences if we consider the fact of choice of SDs. I have often heard from SD participants that they are not interested in mathematical topics but that they always are interested in 'ethical' ones. Is that really so? If it was, then it would be impossible for them to decide between two 'ethical' topics, say on the eve of an SD week. But it isn't impossible; in fact, it is very often quite easy. So not everybody has the same kinds of interest in all so-called 'ethical' questions. This has to do, I think, with the different kinds of people we are, with the different values and combinations of values each of us embodies.

§ 19   In other words, there is not a realm of values within which we could distinguish 'ethical' values that are universal and 'non-ethical' values that only concern some particular people (e.g. mathematicians). There is only one realm of values; and each of us partakes only of a small portion of it. Which values are my values means what kind of person I am, what kind of life I live. And no human life can encompass all values. But we can still share a little bit of what underlies another human life by means of the SD. We can still listen to the voices of different gods, as it were. That is, we can *if we care to do so*. The SD is one of the most extraordinary inventions ever devised to share in other people's lives and listen to those voices.

§ 20   Summing it all up, I would like to say that every SD is about ethics *because every SD is about human lives*. Which was exactly the point Socrates himself made again and again when he said that he examined lives, not just words.

Post Loccum Scriptum

§ 21 As part of our preparation for the plenary session at the Loccum conference, in which the presentations made by Jos Kessels, Horst Gronke and myself would be discussed, we three carried out an inquiry, a kind of SD, to clarify our positions. The main result of our inquiry was that each of us is asking a different question, so there is no wonder that we appear to contradict each other or at least to say wildly different things. There is no actual contradiction, it transpired after the proceedings, but we *are* saying wildly different things; and the reason is simply that we are trying to answer very different questions. Jos's question is about *possibility:* how can we conduct a SD in a particular setting, viz. within an organisation? Horst's question, again, is about *obligation:* how should we conduct a SD no matter what the setting is? My own question, finally, is about *empirical fact:* how do we conduct SDs in different settings? Consequently, although each one of us is inquiring about the relationship between ethics and SD, our questions are different and hence our answers, too, are different:

(1) Jos Kessels is saying, basically, that when we conduct SDs within organisations, there are strict constraints as to how far we can talk in ethical terms. Not having the slightest experience of a SD in an organisation myself, I defer to Jos's superior knowledge of what happens in such settings, although I would query his distinction between ethical and non-ethical terms. For I don't think that distinction can be clearly drawn (§ 12; see also § 22).

(2) Horst is saying, basically, that no matter in what setting we conduct a SD, there are certain ethical requirements we are supposed to honour. I agree with that, although I am not sure that he, or anybody else for that matter, is in a position to say exactly what those requirements are. The SD is not a technique; so, even if we can up to a point set forth the rules for SD (including "ethical" rules, if they are indeed distinct from non-ethical ones, which I doubt), at some point we have to stop. To know how to conduct, facilitate or participate in, an SD is a matter of practice and experience, not a matter of rules. Sometimes that practice and experience seems limited to actual SDs and does not seem to spill over to other conversations (see § 25).

(3) I am saying, basically, that, as far as my experience of SD reaches, we are always engaging in an exploration of values, whether those are the values of the facilitator (most conspicuous in so-called mathematical SDs) or the values of the example-giver (most conspicuous in so-called ethical SDs). Sometimes, we even explore the values of one or several of the other participants, but such exploration is necessarily very restricted, for time never allows for more than marginal attention to it (see § 23). This is so as a matter of empirical fact, at least in my personal experience. It would be great if some form of empirical (psychological, sociological, ethnographic, linguistic) research could be done on SDs to find out more of other people's experience of how SDs are actually conducted (see § 24).

§ 22 Both before, during and after the conference in Loccum some people challenged my view that SDs are all about ethics. They particularly insisted that a mathematical SD could not possibly be about ethics. They even said that the example I used in my oral presentation, viz. the possibility of having a SD on music (which, because it was a SD, would be about ethics as well) was ill-chosen. I am not going to repeat their arguments, because, whatever their merit, they did not address my main point, viz. that there is no way in which we can distinguish satisfactorily between ethical and non-ethical values (§ 12; see also § 16). Nevertheless, the sheer resistance of so many people against using the word "ethics" in such a broad sense has taught me a lesson. This broad sense is indeed the original Greek sense (a matter I don't want to argue here); but meanings change, so maybe I should drop the word "ethics". In fact, I am prepared to do so and to change the thesis of this paper to "Every SD is about values no matter what its subject matter", as long as this is taken to imply that *all* kinds of values are concerned in a SD — and that *all* kinds of value have a role to play in how an individual lives his or her life. If that were understood, then I'd be happy to drop the word "ethics"; for nothing important ever hinges on a word.

§ 23 Another objection I have often heard is that my interpretation of SD assigns too important a role to the example-giver, to the detriment of the other participants. (This is to the exclusion of mathematical SDs, which do not ordinarily have an example-giver in the same sense. See §§ 14-19.) I am guilty as charged. However, I would like to remind the reader that, when I do what I am accused of doing, I am not recommending that the example-giver *should* have such a role. My thesis is not about how SDs should be conducted; it is only about how they *are* in actual fact conducted, as far as my experience reaches (§ 1, § 21). In all SDs I have participated in, or indeed facilitated, the example-giver *does* play a central role, for we are trying to find out about her values. Do we thereby marginalize the other participants? In a sense we do; for there is not enough time to explore all values of all participants (or even all values of that one participant who is offering us the example). In another sense we don't. Just think for a minute what we do as participants: we try to listen to what the example-giver is telling us; we ask questions about the example, about how she felt, about why she did what she did, and so on. We are *examining her life*, to use Socrates' wonderful expression (§ 20). I don't think this is in detriment of the other participants; in fact, I think it does them a lot of good. The only reason I can think of why anybody should think that by assigning an absolutely central role to the example-giver we are somehow trespassing over other people's rights is that we are culturally conditioned to value speaking more than listening. But that is exactly the point for me: the SD is different from other kinds of conversation precisely because we listen more. Whether in fact we really listen *enough*, that's another question (see § 25).

§ 24 During the Loccum conference there was a poster session in which Peter Rickman made a presentation. I was busy co-conducting another poster presentation somewhere else, so I couldn't attend that particular one. But from what I have heard and read, and from conversations with Peter himself, I think he is issuing a real challenge to SD. His main question is this: Could the search for consensus be counterproductive in that it would almost inevitably lead to trivial agreements on widely shared prejudices? This is not the place to elaborate on this question, and I am not going to try. Yet by thinking about it I came to the conclusion that one way of conducting research on what the SD is and what it does to people (§ 1) would be to apply to it the framework of cognitive social psychology known as "implicit theories". This is a field of research in which people are trying to find out what sorts of conceptions, models or theories people develop more or less spontaneously. We know now, for instance, that the conceptions people have about the physical or the biological world are a hindrance to their proficient learning of physics and biology at school. Those conceptions do not usually exist in an articulated form; in fact, they are difficult to articulate; but they guide the way we act and the way we think about the world. In a similar fashion, psychologists are also trying to find out about "implicit theories" relating to the social and cultural world. Now SD is a unique place in which people are trying hard to articulate their deepest conceptions and values. Hence a collaboration between SD and research on "implicit theories" could prove very fruitful for both.

§ 25   At the Loccum conference we all witnessed, I think, a repeat of what some of us had already experienced at the Leusden conference: a failure to conduct a proper dialogue on the differences emerging between SD practice in Germany and in the Netherlands. I am not interested in saying here what I think about this controversy, nor would this be the right place to do it. But it was a very sad thing to watch. It is sad, because we are all engaged in SD, we are all trying to find out what it is and how we could improve its practice; yet people who should know better, who are supposed to be proficient practitioners of SD, do not seem to have absorbed the most elementary cultural practice of SD, which is to listen to what the other person is trying to say, to meet her halfway, to ask what she means instead of assuming you know what she means, and so on. I started this paper by saying that nobody knows what SD is and that the only way to know that is by doing some empirical research (§ 1). Well, one of the questions often asked about SD is whether and how far it changes people (hopefully, for the better). Some old hands have suggested that they have been changed by SD, that they have become better listeners and less ready to overtrump the other person. I believe them. But what we saw at Loccum (and before that, at Leusden) was not a good example of that. If people who have done dozens and dozens of SDs, who have even successfully facilitated them, cannot practice its virtues when they are most needed, then this is not good evidence that SD is actually capable of changing people.

Gisela Raupach-Strey

Searching for Truth versus Practical Application?

The heading question was not put by myself; 'searching for truth' and 'practical application' are not on the same level and therefore they aren't a real opposition. This is what I shall try to show in several respects, above all in the tradition of critical philosophy. First I subsume the opposition of 'searching for truth' and 'practical application' to the opposition of theory and practice.

I. An old problem: victory versus truth

(1) The problem that was discussed in our organizations (for instance in Leusden in 1998) and which led to the heading question is not a new one. We find it already in classical antiquity with Socrates and the sophists. Socrates strove for insight into truth and helped his dialogue partners to reach this aim following a process of arguments, whereas Protagoras taught them rhetoric to win legal proceedings (in return for money). Protagoras was reproached by Socrates for persuading instead of convincing; it is a conflict between power and truth. An example: you can try to be declared innocent and may be successful even if you are guilty; so it is another question whether you are guilty and, at the very least, there is the question 'what is guilt?'

(2) For Socrates 'truth' is not particular, but fundamental, universal and eternal; not transitory practice and not outer appearance, but timeless and essential. The implicit recognition theory of Socrates was explained by Plato in his parable of the cave with the 'intuition of ideas', which is only possible because everybody has seen the ideas before being born. Nevertheless truth is existential too,

concerning human life. The dialogues of Socrates begin with questions which arise out of everyday experience. They are significant for life, let us say, when they lead to uncertainty about former convictions, or to unconvenient conclusions — remember Socrates accepting the capital sentence. The reasons, for example, for fulfilling a promise, are general, and practical application to a concrete situation involves acting according to reasonable insight. So truth is taken seriously both in a logical-reasonable and in a moral sense. 'Recognizing ourselves' is the motto of philosophizing in a Socratic manner; the universal truths, which surmount the individuum, are a mirror and a measure which no individual is allowed to overbear for reasons of situation or opportunity. Truth has practical consequences for men and women, it is not suitable for exercising power over human beings like objects.

II. Historical aspects of this idea of truth

(1) In the history of the Occident we find priority is given to the 'vita contemplativa' over the 'vita activa' — contemplation and reflecting over working for everyday-life and business. It was the ideal of Plato as well as of the medieval monasteries and convents, for which the 'unio mystica' was the paramount aim. Even in modern times you find the opinion that science has nothing to do with values.

(2) Apart from this hierarchy of forms of life there have been and there are other aspects of the opposition 'theory-practice' and other tendencies:

a) Plato himself wanted philosophers to govern the state; similarly Aristotle attributed to them the function of the 'steersman' because of their overview into what is essential. That means: the theoretical form of life, which was regarded as the highest, implicated practical obligations.

b) 'ora et labora' was the main rule of the Benedictine-monks; that means spiritual life and working and caring for secular necessities belong together, they form a unity of theory and practice. In this context 'practice' is, in a certain sense, a verfication of faith.

c) Attributed to Meister Eckhart I found a sermon interpreting the story of Mary and Martha (in Luke 10, 38-42) not in the obvious way of estimating Mary's adoration for the words of Jesus, but increasing the value given to the activity of Martha, whose caring household had — according to the interpreter — already passed Mary's stage.

d) Modern sciences have turned to the reality which can be experienced; they are grounded on practical activities of observation and experiment.

e) In various theories of revolution, theory only gives the motivation and the impulse to change social reality; changing bad social conditions into human conditions is regarded as the highest aim.

f) The philosophy of the 20th century is occupied with problems of this concrete world, for instance in politics and in medical ethics.

g) In the present, we find the ideal of the busy 'business man'; rarely the old ideal of erudition.

III. Links between theory and practice within the philosophical theory of recognition

It would take too much space here to follow all lines of the relation between theory and practice in the history of modern philosophy. Let us have a look at an important line of the theory of recognition.

(1) Kant has not only written a 'critique of pure reason', but also two other critiques: of 'practical reason' and of 'judgement'. The latter builds a bridge between notion and perception; it is the capacity which enables us to judge about practical situations referring to universal principles. In a variation of a famous sentence of his we can say: theory without practice is empty, practice without theory is blind.

(2) Nelson focussed on the way in which universal principles are uncovered through the process of reflecting. He analysed this process of how universal principles can be recognized using the method of 'regressive abstraction'. It is, so to speak, an 'inductive'

method, beginning with spontanous judgements about practical situations, progressing to the principles underlying them and making them certain through argument.

(3) In the tradition of critical philosophy, in which the efforts of Kant and Nelson are combined, theory and practice form a unity of cognitive process and results. 'Practice' in this context means the material for discovering universal principles just as much for applying them.

Therefore, regarding the cognitive level of the terms in opposition as well as their working together, we can say, that the separation of theory and practice in the heading question is not justified.

IV. Links between theory and practice in ethics: 'practice' also means doing something with respect to ethical norms

In the tradition of Kant and Nelson, but also of Socrates, 'practice' also has another meaning: acting in our world of life, with free decision and obligated to moral principles as a guide.

(1) In Aristotle's concept of virtue we find, perhaps for the first time, this turn to behaviour in everyday life.

(2) 'Searching for truth' in ethics means finding out what rule is valid in general. Kant provided the theoretical basis for this. According to his 'categorical imperative' the ethical norm has to be universal. No exception of any kind is allowed. Practical situations are cases, which have to be judged according to what is valid in general. So we have in ethics a similar relation between theory and practice as in recognition theory: We cannot think the one without the other.

(3) Practical application involves judging human behaviour and acting according to theoretical, reasonable norms. Kant rejects the idea that practice should be ruled by other laws than theory.

(4) According to Nelson (as well as Socrates and Kant) we are obliged to do what, by reflection, we have recognized as valid. In so far as practice has to be understood and guided by reason, it is the same relation regarded from the other side. But Nelson took a very strong

motivation out of his ethical thought. Sometimes in reading his books I have the impression that he feels his philosophizing is only justified when he puts his insights into practical steps: in everyday life, in paedagogy, in politics. Here we find a further, very narrow link between theory and practice: submitting all thinking and doing to a high moral standard.

The above were only some outlines concerning the relation of theory and practice. But concerning epistomology as well as ethics my conclusion is the same: the question has not been put in an appropriate way.
Refining the heading question I give it this form:

V. Does Socratic Dialogue belong to the Platonictradition of the priority of theory?

The answer depends on the point of view we are taking:
(1) In a cognitive sense this is true. In Socratic Dialogues we are searching for basic insights, which are not particular, but generally valid. Limited insights are not reallly satisfying since it is always possible to progress from the particular to the universal. The claim for universalism is a criterion for the Socratic method as well as for philosophizing in general. In this sense 'truth' is a regulative ideal, which guides our imperfect reflections.
(2) In respect to the form of life, it is not true. Socrates, Kant and Nelson, as representatives of the Enlightenment, wanted to clarify issues concerning everyday life (individual and political) in our concrete world. Their aim was not to escape into the ivory tower of theory, but to recognize the conditions and principles under which humans could live autonomously. They also stressed acting: Kant wanted the public to enlighten itself. And Nelson vehemently wanted to see philosophy becoming practical, in paedagogical as well as in political life, and he was very active in furthering this idea. The PPA is linked to this tradition.
(3) Concerning the method, theory and practice refer mutually to each other: The analysis of examples of everyday experience leads into insight into truth. Searching for truth assists human beings in their

self-education, and the development of their autonomy and responsibility. The goal is understanding concrete reality with help of abstract concepts — the 'Socratic Principle' according to Gustav Heckmann.

In all forms of enlightenment we have this knowledge about timeless truths, but at the same time no turning away from the world, but a turning to the world as it is. The claim for enlightenment has always been a motor of critical philosophy, of awareness about social and political developments and of engagement in paedagogical and political contexts.

Therefore the presupposition of self-sufficiency of theory is not legitimate concerning Socratic Dialogues: searching for truth serves practical application, whereas focussing practice illustrates abstract notions and theoretical sentences, and both are ending in a practical engagement.

VI. Problems

(1) The mutual relationship of theory and practice that I pointed out in the paragraphs before, must not be interpreted in such a way that the paramount aim of Socratic method would be over-shadowed by application to the concrete world. Searching for truth is constitutive for Socratic Dialogue; its application to real life situations is a part of the searching process and should not be put in opposition to it in a wrong way.

(2) Two sorts of dialogue should be distinguished:

a) dialogues 'without purpose', i.e. their only aim is insight and self-education, not practice in an immediate sense;

b) dialogues under given conditions and serving certain purposes, especially as an instrument for making decisions.

Originally Socratic Dialogues belong to the first category. As soon as they are used in the second way, for other purposes than search for truth, problems arise. Especially, we have to be aware of the danger of Socratic Dialogues being instrumentalized. That would be the case, if somebody has the opinion: 'It is more important that the workers of our firm like to work with us again after the Socratic Dialogue, than that they find out the true reasons of their discontentment.'

(3) The boundary is not always that sharp, particularly in all sorts of school situations: in teaching philosophy and ethics, and in political education. In such contexts there are limitations given through the institutions and/or through paedagogical aims.

For example, to my mind bringing Socratic Dialogues into teacher training is very useful, but surely the Socratic method is even here a little bit 'used' for other aims (for opening the mind, for listening to each other, for formulating own thoughts, for emancipation, etc.). We never discussed dangers which are lying in institutional teaching practice, even if there are dangers. On the other hand, these aims only stress isolated aims belonging to the search for truth, they don't contradict it.

Bringing Socratic Dialogues into economic or consulting contexts, the limitations and possible abuse appear to me even more weighty. One reason is that of the non-ideal conditions of the Socratic Dialogue itself, which cannot be discussed in such contexts without serious consequences, at least there are limitations to discussing this.

VII. My proposition to solve these problems

For a Socratic Dialogue to be Socratic it is not necessary that they are so-called 'pure' Socratic Dialogues following only a cognitive interest. This hidden reproach would be not only a theoretical misunderstanding, but also a contradiction to the practical tradition of Socratic Dialogue after Nelson. Rather the relation is important between the intention of 'searching for truth' and other intentions:

(1) The other intentions must be compatible with the intention 'searching for truth'; they are not legitimate, when they contradict the 'logos-principle' or the reasonable self-determination of the dialogue partners.

(2) Even if the intentions are compatible, we have to ensure that other intentions don't override searching for truth; that means: we have to weigh up the different sorts of purposes.

(3) And we have to recognize the social and political conditions under which we offer Socratic Dialogues. It is not acceptable to avoid critical reflection about these preconditions.

Socratic Dialogue can well be used in all aspects of life; in the tradition of critical philosophy it is even a duty to do so. But we have to be aware that the aim can be displaced or even falsified. Whenever and wherever we are practising Socratic method, we have to listen to the warnings of Socrates. Philosophizing is not a matter of convenience.

Socrates determined discourse rules which are essential: we should not be concerned with what people say, what emotions we have or what may be disadvantageous consequences we expect for our life. We are not tied to particular aims, we have to respect only truth and reasonable arguments for truth ('logos-principle').

By contrast, the more you are paid, the more you have to consider the interests at stake, rather than the reasons. Socratic skill has its value in itself and is unpayable in this sense. That doesn't mean that Socratic Dialogues in 'non-pure' contexts should be forbidden — Let me point out again: it is even our responsibility to make them fruitful in different social contexts. But we need to be aware that they don't become instrumentalized for secondary purposes and cease to be Socratic compared not only with the ideas of Nelson and Heckmann, but also compared with the dialogue rules of Socrates himself. We should keep these rules in our mind as a valuable measure to deliberation. There are a lot of dangers in missing the true meaning of Socratic Dialogue, and everybody who uses this determination is called to realize this meaning for the best he/she can in a responsible manner and in the spirit of critical thinking.

Papers

Jos Kessels

Beyond Appearances:
Plato's Myth of the Cave Revisited

Introduction

The British novelist and philosopher Iris Murdoch investigated Plato's ideas about art and metaphor in relation to the Socratic ideal and philosophy in general. Her studies indicate that a Socratic dialogue is not to be understood as a scientific inquiry, because the knowledge we are after in such a dialogue is generally of a much more personal and literary type than in science. The ascent of knowledge, outlined in Plato's myth of the cave, implies not only an increase in cognitive precision (conceptual and perceptual), but also in affective and sociodynamic precision. This entails that dialectic needs to reserve a much bigger role for non-rational elements and non-expressibles, like images, than philosophers have tended to admit.

This paper gives, on the basis of a concrete example of a Socratic dialogue, a survey of some of Plato's and Murdoch's ideas, leading to a different interpretation of what we are doing in a Socratic dialogue from the traditional neo-Kantian one established by Nelson and Heckmann. From this interpretation some new types of Socratic questions and dialectic interventions follow, which are presented and discussed.[1]

Setting and starting question

Last year I conducted a series of Socratic Dialogues in an adult education program of a large Dutch banking firm, the Rabobank. Originally an

---

1   I would like to thank Erik Boers, Pieter Mostert and Dick Elstgeest for their valuable comments on this article.

agricultural co-operative, a farmers loan bank, it is not exclusively a farmers bank anymore, but a general bank, one of the biggest in Holland. Yet it has preserved its co-operative business form. This implies that all the offices of the bank are formally autonomous organizations, with a director of its own, a board of management and a supervisory board. At the same time, however, all offices are part of the national and international umbrella organization, which provides them with all sorts of staff services, general directives and guidelines. This creates a natural tension between on the one side loyalty and compliance to the larger organization, and, on the other, the need for enough elbow-room for individual decisions and private policies. It is, in short, the tension between autonomy and co-operation. It was this tension the participants in the Socratic Dialogue wanted to investigate. They formulated it in the starting question: how far does autonomy extend in the co-operative?

The participants at the dialogue were all directors of a bank or members of the management team. They followed a 2.5 year Master of Business Administration course set up by Nyenrode University, a Dutch business school, especially for the Rabobank. In the first year of their study they took part in a series of Socratic Dialogues. Inclusion of Socratic Dialogues in the programme served essentially two educational objectives: training in visioning (analysing experiences in terms of a broader, more fundamental view) and training in dialogical skill (dialectic). The series of dialogues comprised six sessions from 16.00 - 19.30 hours, including a snack or a small meal. In these six sessions participants inquired into three questions, one question being dealt with in two sessions. All starting questions were selected by the participants. In accordance with the normal Socratic methodology in the Nelson-Heckmann tradition, every first session was dedicated to an exploration of the question, finding concrete examples, selecting one example for further analysis, describing the example and starting the analysis. Then in between the first and the second session everyone did homework, summarizing the example, transpositioning (putting themselves in the position of the example-giver), taking a stand themselves and describing their personal arguments. In the second session we investigated the several positions and arguments and tried to reach a joint answer to the original question.

The example

In one group, of six participants, someone came up with the following example.[2] Some years ago six offices of the bank in his region decided to create a joint platform for 'housing and mortgages'. In several places in their region large building projects for new residential areas were planned. By developing a coherent policy as to rates, lending conditions and the like, and by presenting themselves as one platform, they would be a better partner for estate agents and other brokers and also for the individual potential buyers. That could give them a bigger share of the market than each of them would be able to obtain by themselves.

The platform was rather successful. Every bank had a fixed delegation in it. After about two years one of the delegates left the platform and was replaced by a new person, due to a fusion of two bank offices. This new man immediately announced that he was not very happy with the whole set up, especially not the arrangement with the estate agents. He felt it restricted his freedom. The others tried to convince him of the advantages of their co-operation, but did not seem to persuade him. He promised, though, to get in touch with the estate agents and brokers in his own town, and inform the others of the results of his consultations.

Shortly after that, however, our example-giver received a telephone call from the manager of a rival bank, who wanted to know why the Rabobank had suddenly reduced its rates and stopped charging commissions. Our example-giver was astonished and had to admit that he could not answer the question. Then before he could find out he got another telephone call from one of the estate-agents, who was furious that the Rabobank had abruptly and unilaterally terminated the arrangement with them. Upon inquiry it appeared that the office of his colleague had without notice or warning stopped its participation in the platform and started autonomous sale-efforts. Representatives of this office approached aspirant buyers personally, in the information centre at the building site, with a letter containing a 'unique offer' of low mortgage rates and no commission if they would come directly to their office, without the intervention of a broker. This led to quite some commotion

---

2   Circumstances have been slightly altered in order to anonimize the case.

in the market. The estate agents, feeling shut out, were so angry that they requested the police to remove the employees of this office from the information centre at the building site.

The next day, between all the rest of the hectic, the participants in the platform had numerous phone calls with one another, to deliberate about the situation. They tried to get in touch with their colleague, but he did not come to the phone nor answered their emails. At the end of the day all banks were compelled to reduce their rates.

Judgement, assumptions, transpositioning

The judgement of our example-giver was clear: in this case the colleague that stepped out of the platform had gone too far. Formally every Rabobank is autonomous, so formally he had the right to do this. But, he said, you cannot just terminate an agreement, break a covenant, and abandon a well-functioning co-operation unilaterally and without giving notice. The least this man should have done was consult some of his colleagues in the platform. Collaborating in a group practice implies accepting at least some obligations, like careful communication, sticking to an agreement and subordinating your own decision process to that of the group as a whole. You cannot just withdraw from all social intercourse and confront your colleagues with 'radio silence', especially not in a co-operative like the Rabobank.

Some of the participants in the dialogue heartily agreed with this judgement, and for the same reasons. But there were doubts too. One person in particular did not think that this man had driven his autonomy too far. He could imagine having done the same thing, if he had been in the same situation as he. After all, the platform was a totally informal happening; nothing of the agreement had been set down in writing, neither internally, nor with outside partners like the estate agents. And circumstances in the market may make a bank change its course, even if you are part of a platform or a co-operative. Wasn't it precisely this autonomy that had always been the strength and the distinctive ability of the bank as a co-operative, its competence to change course swiftly when they felt it necessary?

Confusion

In the next part the dialogue got entered into a phase of confusion. First the group talked about when or how a participant in the platform should be allowed to quit. What procedures were appropriate when you worked with a tacit covenant, one that is not fixed in written rules? Then someone objected that this was a different question from the original one, how far autonomy extends in the co-operative. Going back to that question the group talked about whether the sudden, unexpected move of this colleague had impaired the common interest, the benefit and well-being of the organization at large. Some thought it had, because it betrayed the confidence of colleagues, of other banks and of the group of estate agents. It thereby harmed the image of the bank. Others in the group did not agree with that. That's just what business is like, they suggested.

One participant brought up that if the Rabobank wants to be a co-operative, then its members should at least share some values, like that you can build on someone's word and that you give first priority to the interests of the clients of the co-operation. Being a member of the co-operative, you would have to keep up these values, also in this situation. But some replied that the bank not only wanted to be a co-operative, but also had the responsibility of being an effective and profitable organization. If these values conflicted with the co-operative values, it might well be possible you would have to choose the organizational ones, as happened in this case. Another participant believed that we were constantly confusing two different questions, the question of how far autonomy extends in the co-operative, and the question of how communication should flow inside the organization. In this case you could very well be distressed about this colleague's lack of communication skills and at the same time contend that he had not gone too far in autonomy. A problem in frank and open communication is a different thing from a problem in autonomy. We had to admit that the man in question certainly knew what he wanted. And you can only create a strong and effective co-operative with highly autonomous people, like him.

Plato's analogy of the cave

Before relating the last part of the dialogue, let us have a look at the theory of Socratic Dialogue. This will give us a chance to compare two diverging interpretations of what is going on here. Plato presented a brief and concise summary of his ideas about the growth and development of knowledge in the form of the famous analogy of the cave (cf. Plato, Republic, VII, 514-520). Since then all sorts of models have been advanced about this topic. Many of them are variants of Plato's scheme.[3] In Plato's analogy the human condition is likened to that of prisoners in a cave. They have been there all their life, fettered at feet and necks, so they cannot get up and turn around. Behind them there is a fire, and between the fire and them there is a wall, above which all sorts of things are carried back and forth, as in a puppet theatre. Since the prisoners have not seen anything else in their life, they regard the shadows of these things, thrown at the wall in front of them by the light of the fire, as the real world.

Now imagine one of the prisoners is unchained and forced to go up the path, so he can see the fire and the things of which before he only saw the shadows. Of course he will at first have great difficulty in seeing these things, because his eyes are not accustomed to the light. And if he is dragged along further up the steep path, out of the cave and into the bright light of the sun, this will be so painful for him that he will resist and struggle against it. Once outside the cave he will again at first be fully blinded by the light of the sun, not capable of seeing any of the things around him. Then bit by bit he will get used to it, first looking at shadows and reflections and the sky at night, and later at the things themselves and finally the sun by day. Then he will find out that the sun is the cause of the seasons and the years and that it governs everything in the visible world. He will be so delighted about this knowledge that he will start pitying his fellow prisoners. But when he returns into the cave to tell them about what he has seen, he will be blinded by the darkness and no longer able to discern the shadows on the wall properly. So they will laugh at him and believe he has spoilt his eyes up there and that it is better not to go up and leave the cave.

---

3   In our time for instance Piaget, Kohlberg, Bloom. Cf. Korthagen & Kessels 1999. Nelson is an explicit follower of Plato.

Such, says Socrates, is our situation. The cave is the visible world; the fire is our sun. Climbing up to see the things outside the cave is the ascent of the soul from the sensible to the intelligible world. And the final stage in the growth of knowledge is getting to see the sun of this world, the Idea of the Good, the one thing that is the cause of everything that is good and beautiful, the ultimate source of truth and knowledge. 'And everyone who wants to act wisely, either in private or in public life, should see her.' (Plato, Republic, VII, 517 c)

In the analogy of the line, which runs parallel to the analogy of the cave, Plato distinguishes four levels in the development of knowledge.[4] The first level is called phantasy (eikasia): the prisoners hold the shadows they see for the real world. Similarly, we often hold our fantasies, conjectures, unreflected images and opinions for reality itself. This 'knowledge' is actually not yet knowledge, it is too unreliable, fragmentary and inconsistent for that. Through the need for more clarity and reliability we may get to the second level: the prisoner is unchained and gets to see the objects of which he formerly only saw the shadows. This level Plato calls belief, conviction or justified opinion (pistis). A Socratic Dialogue aims primarily at the development of this type of knowledge. In contemporary language we designate it with terms like 'mental scheme' or 'cognitive model'. At this level we are increasingly capable of describing a phenomenon, perceiving distinctions, explaining and accounting for an opinion. However, this knowledge is still attached to sensory experience and concrete situations, that is to say, it is still relative and changeable.

Then the prisoner climbs out of the cave, into the daylight, to see for the first time the world as it really is. This transition from the second to the third level is the hardest one. It is the transition from being satisfied with a relative, changeable, situation-bound opinion, to really wanting to know what a thing is. At this level, which Plato indicates with the term 'dianoia' and which we usually characterize as theorizing or theory formation, sensory reality and its cognitive schemes are considered to be the manifestation of a deeper reality, an underlying 'form'. We call it the essence of a thing, the structure or law of it, the pattern or system, that which stays the same in a continuously changing reality and which creates unity in the multitude of appearances. Clearly at this level knowledge is

---

4   Plato, Republic, VI, 509-511. Cf. Reeve 1988, Korthagen/Kessels 1999.

abstracted from experience, definitions and principles are formulated and logical relations are clarified. By doing that we produce an order of mental schemes in an abstract language. This is the level where mathematics is situated, knowledge that is stable, unchangeable and consistent.

On top of that Plato distinguishes a fourth level (noèsis): the prisoner sees the sun itself, the source of all light and life. This is the ultimate level of truth and goodness, the final knowledge, the immediate vision of the Forms or Ideas. It is the level of absolute, transcendent, spiritual values, that cannot be articulated, but only directly seen and experienced. 'It cannot be put in words, but through prolonged, dedicated, scientific dealings with the subject and an intimate acquaintance with it, suddenly it appears in the soul, as a light that is kindled through a jumping spark, and then it feeds itself from itself.' (Plato, Letters VII, 341 c,d.)[5]

Locating the dialogue in Plato's scheme

Now where in this scheme do we have to locate the dialogue I described? At what level of knowledge is the group working? And what would the group have to do to ascend further on the scale of knowledge? What can a Socratic facilitator, a stand-in for Socrates, do to stimulate further progress?

I will not go deeply into the first two questions. For a precise account of the level of knowledge that the group is working on we would have to dig much deeper into the details of the dialogue.[6] I will assume that the group is working at the second level: it is trying to form from different private and unreflected (or not thoroughly reflected) opinions a common justified opinion, an argued standpoint, a joint mental scheme. The problems it experiences with respect to the content of the dialogue have to do with clarifying what exactly happened in the example, and how precisely this relates to the starting question and the crucial concepts

---

5   Cf. Nelson 1970, p. 271 (Die sokratische Methode).

6   Cf. Kessels & Korthagen 1996 for an analysis of different types of knowledge, and Korthagen & Kessels 1999 for a detailed account of the levels and the transitions between them from a contemporary educational perspective.

'autonomy' and 'co-operative'. This results in a repeated sharpening of the starting question, distinguishing between what needs to be investigated and what not. The group is in the middle of this complex and laborious process.

Instead I will concentrate here on the last two questions: what would the group have to do to ascend further on the scale of knowledge? And what can a Socratic facilitator do to stimulate such progress? According to the Nelson-Heckmann type of dialectical practice, what both the group and the facilitator need to do here is: just go on with the process of clarifying the relevant facts and concepts, in order to be able at some point to formulate a proper and commonly accepted regressive syllogism, or a series of such syllogisms. A regressive syllogism would be for instance an argument of the form:

- this man went too far (judgement, conclusion),
- because he acted autonomously though he was bound by co-operative agreements (factual, minor premise),
- and one is not allowed to act autonomously when bound by co-operative agreements (normative, major premise, rule).

Though this is without further clarification a much too indefinite and global syllogism, it can illustrate what we aim for in the Nelson-Heckmann Socratic Dialogue: beginning with a judgement, which is supposed to be the conclusion of an argument, we try to find the proper formal structure of the argument that makes the conclusion intelligible. The syllogism is called *regressive* because, in distinction to the regular syllogism in which two premises lead up to a conclusion, here the conclusion comes first in the investigation, in the form of an intuitive judgement. This judgement is supposed to 'contain' the premises, i.e. to be built upon assumptions that are partly or wholly tacit. The process of investigation is meant to make explicit what these premises are, working back from the conclusion to the underlying premises, and testing these assumptions for validity. The premises are partly factual or descriptive (minor premises), partly conceptual and normative (major premises), thus making up an appropriate formal syllogism or a series of syllogisms.

It will be clear that an inquiry that leads to the formulation of a regressive syllogism is in fact a double process of analysis and synthesis. It implies not only scrutinizing the example by breaking it down into its relevant constituents, but also enriching the understanding of it by finding its proper form, its intelligible structure. Thus the Socratic analysis aims at finding the logical connection or pattern of connections among the constituents of the example-situation, both descriptively, the reasoned fact, and normatively, the reason why (cf. Byrne 1997, Nelson 1970, pp. 219-246). By further abstracting the reasons from the particulars of the example we arrive at the principles of our thought in a certain question. That's why it is called regressive *abstraction*.

This picture of what happens in a Socratic Dialogue is in full accordance with Plato's analogies about the ascent of knowledge, especially with the mathematical status of his third level of knowledge. For to be able to formulate a proper regressive syllogism like the one above — or a string of syllogisms, or some other formal pattern of intelligible connections — and reach consensus about it, a group must reach a high level of precision and exactness, not only about the relevant facts, but also about how to interpret the starting question, about the definitions of the terms 'autonomy' and 'co-operative', about background opinions concerning vision, aim and strategy of the organization, about the best way to set up or continue the investigation etc. Thus, around a single topic of attention a whole axiomatic order starts crystallizing, a system of principles, theorems and rules of inference. Only here it is not a purely symbolic axiomatic order, like in mathematics and logic, but a moral and epistemological one too.

Also, this picture leads to the conception of Socratic *technè* or dialectic, and thereby of the task of the Socratic facilitator, with which practitioners of the Socratic Dialogue in the Nelson-Heckmann tradition are so well acquainted. What both the group and the facilitator in this picture must do is follow the regular steps of the Socratic Method: examine the question, select an example, find the judgement of the example giver, find the assumptions underlying this judgement. Next the other participants are to put themselves in the position of the example giver, give their judgements and assumptions, search for precision both in facts and reasons, and pursue consensus, thus building up the regressive syllogism or the pattern of intelligible connections that is to give the answer to the starting question. (This is the regular methodology represented in the hourglass-model: question → example → judgement → rules → principles (cf. Kessels 1997).)

Objections to this conception

However, there are some grave problems with this picture of what we do in a Socratic Dialogue. I do not mean here the numerous practical problems that we are confronted with in every Socratic inquiry — like having to tolerate long periods of confusion, or dealing with the many subsequent problems arising at the meta-level, impatience, irritation, personal differences and various other frictions —, neither the fact that we never seem to achieve what we set out to achieve. (To be frank, in 15 years of Socratic Dialogue I never experienced a consensus of the ideal mathematical type outside mathematics groups. Nor did Socrates, for that matter, in Plato's dialogues. One always gets stuck somewhere, perhaps in an interesting and rewarding way, but stuck all the same.) These objections concern only the practical side.

There are more basic, fundamental objections. One is, in clarifying the intelligible structure of the example and searching for its proper form in the light of a specific question, are we doing anything more than unravelling and systematizing our most cherished prejudices? How do we know that, in forming the regressive syllogism, we are not only arranging our dearest fantasies, our beloved biases and common inclinations in a more satisfactory scheme: more explicit, more consistent, based on better reasons, more sharply formulated etc., but deceptions all the same? If that is the case, we actually never reach beyond appearances, never attain to real knowledge, never really get out of the cave. We may be seeing the flickering of the fire, in the terminology of the cave analogy, but not the steady daylight and surely not the sun, the source of light.

Another problem, connected to the previous one, is that this project, of finding the intelligible structure of an example and its proper form or syllogistic structure as an answer to a fundamental question, may completely fail to hit the heart of the problem, the essence of what needs to be inquired into, by being too dry, too barren, too verbal and abstract, too much logic and thinking, too much head stuff. Was not Plato's whole endeavour, in the 'Republic', based on the idea that reason, the head, is to be integrated with ambition, the heart, and pleasure, the belly, to achieve proper balance in the whole, both in an individual person and in 'the person at large', the state? And was the pilgrimage from appearance to reality in the myth of the cave not to be considered as a therapy of the soul? Was it not the task of dialectic to perform that therapy by overcoming illusion, personal fantasy and self-indulgent day-dream, and replacing them by a contemplation of the real world? But then, how could this task possibly be performed if we give (both in theory and in practice) all our attention to the logos-part of the dialogue and leave out the heart and the belly? If these are valid objections, we need to inquire what we can do to satisfy our need for spirit and vivacity and enjoyment in a Socratic Dialogue. What instruments on the affective and the sociodynamic level does a Socratic facilitator have, in addition to the cognitive ones, that may be equal to this task?

Murdoch's analysis

It is for these two objections, that I would like to introduce some ideas of the British novelist and philosopher Iris Murdoch. In a series of essays on Plato she gave an analysis of the predicament that the Socratic/Platonic project arrived at in our age (Murdoch 1999). According to Murdoch, the main problem in much contemporary moral thinking is that reason is construed on a scientific model, in a language that tries to be impersonal and universal in its exactness. Hence being moral is reduced to an impersonal competence as well, namely to seeing accurately the relevant facts and the relevant reasons for acting, leaving out all personal and non-rational elements. Similarly, both individual and group are considered as highly conscious self-contained beings, capable of choosing their reasons in freedom and acting upon them. Neither their attitude, nor the quality of their attention, nor the way they deal with emotions are supposed to play a role. It is exactly this objectivity, this exclusion of personal and affective features, that moral reason is thought to require. In fact the individual is reduced to a pure will, operating in an isolated way, and therefore prey to experiences of void, that are either explained as an indication that we are free in relation to reasons, as Kantians do, or as an indication that there are no ultimate reasons, as existentialists do. As a logical consequence of all this, the task of philosophy itself, inquiring into human nature, is reduced to a highly specialized, intellectual activity, namely finding 'a set of terms in which ultimate judgements of value can be very clearly stated'. (Murdoch 1999, p. 335)

Murdoch believed this whole picture of moral philosophy to be essentially mistaken. She did not seem to be acquainted with Nelson's line of neo-Kantianism, but all her points fit Nelson's philosophy remarkably well. And obviously they lead to the conception of Socratic technè described above, in which the aim of a Socratic Dialogue is to find within the framework of a specific question some 'ultimate judgements of value' that are 'very clearly stated', namely a string of regressive syllogisms that clarifies the logical pattern of connections among the constituents of the example situation in such a way that a clear and distinct answer to the starting question can be given.

Murdoch's alternative view: A different exactness

But moral reason cannot be construed on a scientific model. Neither can inquiring into moral reason, for instance through a Socratic Dialogue, be interpreted as a scientific or purely intellectual inquiry. The idea that the real problems of human life or our basic thoughts about human destiny can be described in the impersonal and universal terminology of science is an error. Such terminology is simply not equipped to deal with the real problems (Murdoch 1999, p. 358).True, the progressive discovery of reality, sketched in the cave analogy, requires the development of an increasing conceptual and perceptual exactness, an increasing accuracy in both seeing the facts for what they really are and distinguishing the relevant reasons for acting, the rules and principles that properly apply to the situation. But the exactness required here is — in all inquiries that do not have a purely mathematical or scientific theme, that is in nearly all Socratic Dialogues — not only an intellectual exactness. It is also and primarily a moral or emotional exactness. Indeed, intellectual exactness, seeing accurately, is in most cases only possible through emotional exactness, i.e. through being able to see things 'justly or lovingly', as Murdoch puts it (Ib., pp. 313, 317). We can only see a person — or a situation, a course of events, a problem involving people etc. — accurately when we look upon him or her with a just or loving eye. Only then can we perceive what is really there to see. The purely objective scientific viewpoint is essentially insufficient for that. It lacks the proper emotional commitment.

So if we want to see a person as he or she really is we need to inquire into the quality of our personal commitment, the many ways in which we may be emotionally attached to this person or this situation, into our private hopes and desires, ambitions and frights, the whole 'tissue of self-aggrandizing and consoling wishes and dreams which prevents one from seeing what is there outside one'. (Murdoch 1999, p. 348) Morality is a form of realism, and its chief enemy is personal fantasy. The ability to perceive reality, to see what is true, is not achieved through bypassing our fantasies, ignoring our sensibilities, denying our emotions and attachments, but precisely through apprehending, understanding and balancing them.

We can see this in the example. As long as the participants in the Socratic Dialogue talk only in the intellectual, quasi-objective way that most dialogues start with — detached, neutral, 'from the head', without bringing in any personal material —, the inquiry does not get very far. Of course the facilitator can ask for emotions, but often that is not enough to adequately clarify everyone's personal commitment. In this case the example-giver did say he felt somewhat frustrated and annoyed. Most of the others said they would have felt the same, some of them talking in big terms of being angry or indignant, others in smaller terms of 'not being amused'. But all these answers remained pretty much at the outside, which is understandable, for it is not easy to describe emotional engagement in a direct way. Nor is a Socratic Dialogue a T-group or a sensitivity training in which emotions are the accepted focal point from the start. (Most bank directors would not want to participate in such a group, I am afraid.) So the question is, what can you do, as a Socratic facilitator, to get the participants not just intellectually, but emotionally involved?

One instrument to increase the personal commitment of the participants and prevent them from staying in a detached observer's role, is to include the here and now in the inquiry. Curiously enough, in many dialogues the question that is being investigated through the joint analysis of an example also plays a direct role in the conversation here and now. In psychology this phenomenon is called parallel processes. For instance, in our dialogue we investigated the question: how far does autonomy extend in the co-operative? But we, as a group, were in a sense a co-operative too. And each of us might be supposed to be autonomous. So we could look at our own interactions in the dialogue to see how far *our* autonomy extended in *our* co-operation in that very moment. Besides, there was one person who did not agree with the judgement of the others: he felt that his colleague in the example had not gone too far. So he represented a divergent point of view in the co-operative attempt to find a common viewpoint. And he maintained his position in the second session, after everyone had clarified and explained their opinion. So what about him? Was he going too far in his autonomy in this co-operative?

He himself did not think so. He felt he was contributing to an interesting exchange of ideas. But interestingly, neither did the others think so. They agreed that his deviating standpoint had worked as a catalyst and they showed respect for his point of view. So here in the dialogue the deviating standpoint of one of the participants was being respected and even appreciated in the group, while in the example the deviating standpoint of the colleague was not. Why was that? One of the participants thought it was because here the person with a differing standpoint was authentically present: 'You know that is what he is like'. Another thought it was because he justified his position, he revealed himself. So, someone concluded, autonomy, in the sense of taking a different position, could be considered tolerable and even valuable as long as it was justified and presented in an authentic way. Let us have a closer look at this conclusion.

Standard of perfection

This surely was not a purely intellectual assertion, like in science. Nor was it a purely emotional one, like in therapy. It was at least a combination, an attempt to formulate relevant reasons strongly coloured by the personal relationships existing in the group. The question is then, of course, whether it is the right combination, the right reasons: if we talk about looking justly and lovingly at a situation, is this what that means? One may have doubts here. For instance, one may suspect that the assertion was induced by the desire to avoid friction, to preserve the friendly atmosphere, to keep away from possible conflict. On the other hand, the members of the group were well enough acquainted with each other and with the Socratic Dialogue not to keep up appearances or evade unpleasant truths. But how can we make sure that at this point we really hit the heart of the matter and do not just arrange our personal habits and shared biases in a more orderly systematic form, without getting beyond the level of appearances?

Murdoch reminds us here of the Socratic idea that somehow deep inside we possess a standard of perfection, which can move and change us 'because it inspires love in the part of us that is most worthy'. (Murdoch 1999, p. 350) Socrates' whole work consisted of interrogating people in order to make them remember this original knowledge. It has a parallel in art: 'the true artist is obedient to a conception of perfection to which his work is constantly related and re-related'. (Murdoch 1999, p. 350) Likewise, in trying to see the situation in our example 'with a just and loving eye' we inevitably work with the idea of perfection, an ideal limit of goodness, of excellence or virtue. 'There exists a moral reality', Murdoch comments, following Plato, 'a real though infinitely distant standard'. (Ib., p. 324) This standard entails the idea of development, of progress towards the ideal. Moral progress is an endless aspiration to perfection, essentially connected with the change of the individual, with reassessing and redefining one's life and identity in comparison to this ideal standard of perfection.

A Socratic facilitator can introduce this standard through the concepts of the virtues (as we actually did). These concepts can be of great help 'to make certain potentially nebulous areas of experience more open to inspection' (Murdoch 1999, p. 346), and they generate a rich and diversified vocabulary for naming aspects of goodness. The basic scheme of the four cardinal virtues is simple. Plato distinguished three centres of motivation in a human being, which all have their own excellence or virtue: the belly aims at pleasure, its excellence is called temperance. The heart aims at honour, it is ambitious and outgoing, and its virtue is courage. The head aims at knowledge and wisdom, its excellence being prudence. And the right balance between these three is called justice, both in an individual person and in a group, organization or state. On the basis of this a Socratic facilitator may for instance ask what in the situation the proper temperance and the proper courage would be, the two emotional virtues, thus giving participants the chance to inquire into their personal attachments in the situation instead of ignoring and bypassing these.

In the dialogue this question induced an investigation of some existent fears, mainly the fear of conflict, of getting annoyed at one's colleague, and the fear of not being appreciated by others or the group. Participants said they liked to be part of the dynamics of the organization: the interaction, the debates, and the co-operation. But this created a delicate web of expectations, including subtle and less subtle ways of reward and punishment, making you high or low, in or out, important or unsubstantial in a group. Autonomy required the courage to maintain your independence within this web of expectations, to speak one's mind without hurting someone, but also without fear of losing goodwill or being shut out. So temperance in one's own expectations, in the need for appreciation, and courage in frankness, were two of the excellences required here.

Obviously in formulating these virtues the content of the dialogue had shifted from the attempt to define autonomy in terms of organizational rules to the attempt to define it in terms of personal attitude. This shift further led to a reappraisal of the original question, how far does autonomy extend in the co-operative. For on the basis of the analysis of virtues it became clear that this question had perhaps not been a very courageous one: in hindsight it seemed now to have been formulated not so much from a positive attitude towards autonomy, the desire to inquire into its significance and vigour, but rather from a negative, somewhat immature attitude, the desire to inquire into what one could do without getting punished or reproved. This was quite an unbalancing discovery, a refutation (elenchus) of much greater impact than the confusion they had experienced before. For if the motivation to investigate this question had indeed been somewhat immature, what could one expect from this whole analysis except further articulations of immaturity?

Personal language and art

Let us have a closer look at this point of the dialogue. The central concept of inquiry is, still, autonomy. But in this phase it is becoming increasingly clear that the attempt to formulate a definition of this concept in purely impersonal language, like organizational rules or abstract principles, does not make much sense. Moral reason cannot be properly construed in an impersonal language. It is something very personal, much more personal than the use of a common language would suggest. The exactness that we aim for in a Socratic Dialogue, is not so much in the precision of the words we use as in the precision of some non-expressibles: the quality of our attention, of our moral feeling or effort, the question whether we are able to look with a just and loving eye or not. 'Words may mislead us, since words are often stable while concepts alter', says Murdoch. 'We have a different image of courage at forty from that which we had at twenty. A deepening process, at any rate an altering and complicating process takes place.' (Murdoch 1999, p. 322) It is this deepening and complicating process that we try to facilitate in a Socratic Dialogue. 'Knowledge of a value concept is something to be understood, as it were, in depth, and not in terms of switching on to some given impersonal network.' So to learn the meaning of a concept like 'autonomy' something else is required than finding its definition and giving it a place in a regressive syllogism, which are usually seen as the main features of Plato's third stage in the ascent of knowledge. For a definition and a syllogism may still completely fail to hit the heart of the problem, the essence of what needs to be inquired. 'Moral language which relates to a reality infinitely more complex and various than that of science is often unavoidably idiosyncratic and inaccessible', says Murdoch. (Ib., p. 326) And if we cannot get access to this idiosyncratic, very personal level all our moral words and propositions stay empty, lifeless and powerless. They have no capacity to stimulate us to lead our lives in their light. The idea that simply through being rational and using ordinary language we can dig up the real meaning of moral words is an illusion, even if we find a consensus definition in the dialogue.

If this is true, if inquiring into value concepts or moral reason is indeed such a subtle process, what can the facilitator of a Socratic Dialogue do to make a group engage in it, to get the participants to investigate themselves on this deep level, as a Socratic inquiry after virtue must do? Here Murdoch's interpretation of Plato differs from most scholars: to be able to go beyond appearances, to proceed further in the ascent of knowledge, we will have to take art as a model, not science. Instead of only searching for a regressive syllogism, for rules, principles and definitions, we would also have to look for an image, a story, a metaphor that can move us and inspire us. Images are ideas formulated in concrete terms instead of abstract general terms. They may manifest a refined perception of both the question and the situation being investigated, by arranging crucial details in an appealing framework of moral imagination. Finding the proper image is exactly that at which art aims. Contrary to science, art is not aiming at abstract, universal, fixed, well-founded, explicit propositions, like a definition or a regressive syllogism. Art aims at a different type of exactness, at 'concrete universals', at a precise discernment of relevant particulars and at putting these into a form or configuration that strikes us, touches us, and thereby motivates us. Only art can capture both the cognitive and the affective subtlety that we need for being really influenced. Only art can give philosophy, or a Socratic Dialogue, its proper emotional precision and make philosophical inquiry an adequate *technè* or method for the investigation of virtue. Only art gives room for the working of the inexpressible. 'Art', says Murdoch, 'like (in Plato's view) philosophy, hovers about in the very fine air which we breathe just beyond what has been expressed.' (Ib., p. 461) Besides, art and moral philosophy are basically the same endeavour. They are fundamentally of the same 'material'. 'Art and morals are (…) one. Their essence is the same. The essence of both of them is love (…) Love, and so art and morals, is the discovery of reality.' (Ib., p. xiv)

Images

We actually experienced the emergence of such an artful way of thinking in the last part of the dialogue. For some of the participants started searching for suitable metaphors that could adequately articulate what was at stake in the dialogue. Of course they did not like the suggestion of being immature in their thinking about autonomy and co-operation. So one aspect of a suitable image had to be a mature, adult attitude. What image would befit that? At first several metaphors came up having to do with warfare (closing the ranks of the warriors to be stronger in the battlefield and being able to deal a blow to the opponents) and sports (being so flexible, skilful and alert as an individual or a team that you outclass the other players). But these images were felt to be unproductive, they were too conventional, too much of a stereotype, to be really motivating. Besides, using them in the organization would arouse a wrong type of involvement, too much coloured by competition, antagonism and rivalry. Then someone introduced the idea of a theatre play, in which all actors had to be at the same time fully autonomous, independent, self-governing *and* cooperative, concentrating on the whole and serving the others. This metaphor they liked better, it nicely fitted in with the bank's originating story, in which autonomy and co-operation had been the main pillars. But theatre was quite far from most people's personal experience, that was a drawback.

Next they investigated the image of piloting a large ship into the harbour, the ship being the project of the platform, aiming at a large amount of new customers for housing- and mortgage-services, and the six members of the housing-platform being the crew of the several pilot-boats that had to guide the ship into a safe haven. The group spent quite some time in specifying this image, even drawing up pictures of it. Finally, in discussing the co-operation and mutual attunement between the pilots someone came up with yet another metaphor, the story of Bartholomew, which both by its content and by the way he told it impressed us most of all the images. It went more or less like this.

Once upon a time there was a woodcutter who had seven sons. All of them helped their father in his craft. They worked hard and the family flourished. But when the sons grew older a moment came that the oldest one wanted to leave his father and start for himself. Father and son had already had some disagreements on this topic when Bartholomew, a blind man well-known for his wisdom (the patron saint of travellers and gypsies) attended their village. The woodcutter asked him for advice. Bartholomew came to his home and spoke to all of the sons individually. He inquired into their ideas about the problem, and found out that most of them wanted to continue in their father's firm, only the oldest one not. After that he gathered all the family together in the courtyard and asked them to collect a bunch of sticks and branches, small ones and big ones, from the workshop. So they did. Thereupon he asked who of the sons wanted to leave. The oldest son said he did. He invited him to take a thick stick and see if he could break it in two. The son was big and strong, with great effort he broke the stick in two. Then he demanded the others to make a bundle of sticks and put a strap around it, which they did, and invited him again to break the bundle in two. The son tried and tried, but he was not strong enough to do it by himself. That is, said

Bartholomew, the difference between working together and working for yourself: 'Together you are stronger. So whatever you do, keep that in mind.'

Everyone was thrilled by this story. It surely seemed to hit the heart of the problem we were investigating, the tension between autonomy and co-operation. I suppose it could have aroused all sorts of comments and reasoning, but somehow, perhaps due to its beauty and simplicity, it did not. Besides, we had spent more than all our time and this seemed a good point to end the dialogue.

Appearance or reality

Afterwards we may wonder, though, whether the last part of the dialogue had taken us further in our inquiry or not. Had these metaphors and images been an advancement of the analysis or not? Had we in searching for them been ascending or descending the ladder of knowledge? Clearly, it had stimulated the dialogue and excited the group. It had given the dialogue an elegant closure instead of letting it end in the middle of various unfinished lines of thought. It had left us, after the last story, with a feeling of common concern about the relationship between autonomy and co-operation, a sort of shared respect in spite of the different views the group had. But what was the status of this feeling? Was it an indication that we were approaching the essence of the question, its deep structure, which not only enlightened our heads but also delighted our hearts? Was it a sign that we were drawing nearer to the truth, that we were gradually getting to see what reality was really like in this example? Or was it an indication of precisely the opposite? Had we been replacing reality by some attractive, soothing but deceptive appearance? Had we been manipulating and embellishing reality with these images, filling up the uncomfortable emptiness of our own needs and desires with a 'reality' that might have been but was not? In short, were we on the track of 'Being', in Plato's terms, of reality as it really is, or only of a being that is thought and construed and hypothesized, an appearance in the guise of truth and precisely therefore so dangerous that Plato banned all arts and artists from his ideal state?

This is a difficult, much contended question. Of course the fact that the reality of these metaphors, the theatre play or the pilot boat or the woodcutter's story, is a desired reality, an object of intention and endeavour, instead of an immediately given reality, may give it a hollow sound in the ears of an outsider. Worse still, as readers of this paper, not having been part of the process, we may be struck mostly by the instructive tone of these images, invoking unbelief by their very desire to be believable and by their obvious intention to influence people. I suppose if that had indeed been the status and function of these metaphors in the dialogue, we would have done better to avoid them and exclude them altogether from the dialogue. For that is precisely the reason that Plato prohibited artists from presenting their crafty spells as reality itself. But as far as I could see this was not their function. True, fiction may create a world of its own, hiding the truth and deceiving the untrained, inattentive eye into some stimulating or consoling illusion. But it also may be an attempt to grasp reality in its true form, a way of conceiving the existing world as it really is, a means for directing concentration to a deeper reality that can only be seen 'at second sight'. Was this not the whole point of the ascent of knowledge, to develop a proper second sight, an eye that is enlightened by the sun and thereby becomes 'sunlike' itself? That is, anyhow, Murdoch's conception of the task of philosophical inquiry. Philosophy should provide 'rich and fertile conceptual schemes which help us to reflect upon and understand the nature of moral progress and moral failure'. (Murdoch 1999, pp. 335-336) Here we had found some of those 'rich and fertile conceptual schemes', and they surely seemed to help us. Let me try as a final point to clarify in what way.

The sun

In the myth of the cave the prisoner at last sees the sun itself, the source of light which reveals to us all things as they really are. This is the idea of perfection, of excellence and virtue, or as Plato called it the idea of the Good. It is a natural producer of order, only in its light can we see that one thing is better than another or that one thing is real and another not. It is also the ultimate source of motivation, only by its warmth, by its inspiring love in us, do we get going. Besides, it is indefinable, it always lies beyond, and it is from this beyond that it exercises its authority (Murdoch 1999, p. 350). Now the easiest available spiritual exercise, aiming at seeing the sun, is the appreciation of beauty in art and nature, says Murdoch. For this, rightly understood, is the checking of selfishness in the interest of the real. 'Art presents the most comprehensible examples both of the almost irresistible human tendency to seek consolation in fantasy and of the effort to resist this and the vision of reality which comes with success'. (Ib., p. 352) As we saw, a necessary condition for achieving the vision of reality is the capacity to love. 'It is in the capacity to love, that is to *see*, that the liberation of the soul from fantasy consists. The freedom which is a proper human goal is the freedom from fantasy, that is the realism of compassion.' (Ib., p. 354)

But if this capacity to love is ultimately more important than the capacity to construct proper syllogisms and definitions, if the quality of our attention and the spirit with which we look upon a situation or inquire into a question are in the end more important than the rational content of our arguments, then the question rises: 'How do we alter and purify that attention and make it more realistic?' (Ib., p 356) 'Are there any techniques for the purification and reorientation of an energy which is naturally selfish?' (Ib., p. 344) We know that religious believers have always had techniques for this. They focus their thought upon a transcendent God, who is a source of energy, of reorientation, of grace, of a supernatural assistance to human endeavour which can overcome the empirical limitations of someone's personality. Murdoch contends that Plato intended his image of the Good to have a similar function. For the image of the Good, as a transcendent magnetic centre towards which love naturally moves, is 'the least corruptible and most realistic picture for us to use in our reflections upon the moral life.' (Ib., pp. 361, 384) 'I think there is a place both inside and outside religion for a sort of contemplation of the Good, not just by dedicated experts but by ordinary people: an attention which is not just the planning of particular good actions but an attempt to look right away from self towards a distant transcendent perfection, a source of uncontaminated energy, a source of *new* and quite undreamt-of virtue … This is the true mysticism which is morality, a kind of undogmatic prayer which is real and important, though perhaps also difficult and easily corrupted.' (Murdoch

1999, p. 383) It seemed to me that in the dialogue we experienced a little of this type of attention. And I suppose that is what helped us most.

Murdoch's philosophical position is truly Socratic. 'Ethics should not be merely an analysis of ordinary mediocre conduct, it should be a hypothesis about good conduct and about how this can be achieved.' (Murdoch 1999, p. 364) In the dialogue we had been attempting to reach such a hypothesis and we had failed, we did not find a joint answer nor a shared metaphor. But we did feel a little of the warmth of the sun and experienced the transformation of our own attention in the dialogue. Perhaps this is what Socrates meant at the end of Plato's 'Meno', when he said that virtue and excellence are neither innate nor can be taught, but that if in a dialogue the proper questions and answers are formulated 'a divine grace' can be implanted in people (Plato, Meno, 99 e-100 a).

References

Byrne, P.H. (1997): Analysis and Science in Aristotle. Albany: State University of New York Press.

Heckmann, Gustav (1993): Das Sokratische Gespräch. Erfahrungen in philosophischen Hochschulseminaren. Frankfurt am Main: dipa-Verlag.

Irwin, T. (1995): Plato's Ethics. Oxford: Oxford University Press.

Kahn, C. H. (1996): Plato and the Socratic Dialogue. The Philosophical Use of a Literary Form. Cambridge: Cambridge University Press.

Kessels, Jos. (1997): Das Sanduhr-Modell. Methodik des Dialogs. In: D. Krohn 1997, pp.71-80.

Kessels, Jos; Korthagen, Fred (1996): The Relationship between Theory and Practice: Back to the Classics. In: Educational Researcher, 25/3, pp. 17-22.

Kessels, Jos; Korthagen, Fred (1999): Linking Theory and Practice. Changing the Pedagogy of Teacher Education. In: Educational Researcher, 28/4, pp. 4-17.

Krohn, Dieter; Neißer, Barbara., Walter, Nora (eds.) (1997): Neuere Aspekte des Sokratischen Gesprächs. Schriftenreihe der Philosophisch-Politischen Akademie, Vol. IV. Frankfurt am Main: dipa-Verlag.

Murdoch, Iris. (1999): Existentialists and Mystics. Writings on philosophy and literature. Edited by Peter Conradi. Middlesex, England: Penguin Books, Harmondsworth.

Especially:
- The Idea of Perfection, pp. 299-336.
- On 'God' and 'Good',pp. 337-362.
- The Sovereignty of Good Over Other Concepts, pp. 363-385.
- The Fire and the Sun: Why Plato Banished the Artists, pp. 386-463.
- Art and Eros: A Dialogue about Art, pp. 464-495.

Nelson, Leonard (1970): Gesammelte Schriften, Vol. 1. Hamburg: Felix Meiner Verlag.

Especially:
- Von der Kunst zu philosophieren, pp. 219-246.
- Die Sokratische Methode, pp. 269-316.

Reeve, C. D. C. (1988): Philosopher-Kings. The Argument of Plato's Republic. Princeton New Jersey: Princeton University Press.

Roochnik, David (1996): Of Art and Wisdom. Plato's Understanding of Techne. Pennsylvania: The Pennsylvania State University Press.

Kopfwerk Berlin
(Jens Peter Brune, Ulrike Gromadecki, Horst Gronke, Bärbel Jänicke, Beate Littig, Volker Rendez, Sabir Yücesoy)

The Methodology of Socratic Dialogue

Regressive Abstraction — How to ask for and find philosophical knowledge

Introduction

Like Socrates, participants in a Socratic Dialogue search for the general knowledge that underlies judgement and action in our private and professional lives. As Plato's Socratic dialogues show, it is not easy to find a route to philosophical knowledge. For philosophical knowledge requires us to ask questions in a way that is extremely different from the practical thinking of our everyday lives. You also have to argue in an unusual way in order to arrive at a qualified answer to these questions.

Facilitating SD is a practice which should closely combine experience-based know-how in performing dialogues with methodological reflections on this experience. Such reflections could take place in the SD itself. Even though it seems to be scarcely reflected upon until now, the idea of a Methodology-Dialogue lies within SD itself and is analogous to the Meta- and Analysis-Dialogues.

Independent of such a Methodology-Dialogue, our Socratic team within the cultural-philosophical initiative *Kopfwerk Berlin* has developed various training modules which are based on experiences in facilitating SD under different conditions and with heterogeneous groups. We think that there are some advantages in keeping methodological reflections out of the inner course of SD: we can focus on crucial aspects, may refer to more than one or two example situations (as common in SD) and are free to contribute theoretical aspects.

In this essay we try to combine methodological reflection with practical exercises in order to deepen our insights into central methodological points and difficult phases of SD, as well as to invite you to take this reading as an opportunity to develop your own training experiences. The basic concept and some of the exercises described below were demonstrated at a methodological workshop at 2002's Newman Conference held in Birmingham, England.

Considering the well-known main steps and phases of SD we start in section one with the task of finding an initial Socratic question that fits both philosophical substance and relevance for our daily life. Section two deals with the problematic points of the example phase followed by a short section three on the phase of analysis and judgement. For the investigation of the process of "regressive abstraction" in section four we give a short theoretical input on the different meanings of "abstraction" and finally we analyse the method of abstraction in an example dialogue.

1. The initial question in Socratic Dialogue

One of the most important characteristics of the Socratic Dialogue is the Socratic question. For Socrates, as Plato presented him to us, it was typical that, unlike his partners in conversation, he could ask the appropriate questions. These were questions about the *general*. Hence, they were not questions about something concrete and particular such as "Who is the wisest man in Greece?" but questions about general principles of human knowledge, e. g. "What is wisdom?"

Nevertheless, beyond the Socratic question there is much more hidden than just this feature. It basically shapes the whole process of the discussion-with-each-other in the Socratic dialogue. Therefore it is very important to think intensively and carefully about the details of the formulation of the initial question.

In his account of experiences in college seminars, Gustav Heckmann, the mentor of the Socratic method after the Second World War, determined the range of questions that can profitably be tackled in Socratic Dialogue.

"In Socratic Dialogue we work with the instrument of reflection about experience which is available to every participant of the dialogue. Hence, questions which can only be answered by means of other instruments are dropped out. Such instruments are: 1. experiments, or observation or measuring in nature or in the lab. 2. empirical inquiries as usual in social sciences. 3. historical studies. 4. psychoanalytical method which aims to uncover the *individual* mental problems of a human being. As far as I can see all questions, the answering of which does not require one of those four instruments, can profitably be tackled in Socratic Dialogue." (Heckmann 1993, pp. 14 f.)

Here Heckmann gives a rather negative definition of Socratic questions: he tells us what they are not. What, however, can be said in a positive sense about the Socratic type of question? Could we also say something about why one Socratic question is better than another? In order to move forward in this area we have undertaken to find out the distinguishing essential characteristics of questions and, drawing upon this analysis, to develop exercises which should serve to find appropriately formulated questions.

"Knowledge seeking questions" and "knowing in advance questions"

Within linguistic and rhetorical research there are a number of investigations concerning the various forms of question. In particular, within the bounds of counselling and consulting the range of variation of questions is regarded as very important. For our purpose, that is to find out the essentials of the *Socratic* question, it is sufficient to emphasise the fundamental difference between just two kinds of questions.

In almost every investigation about questions there is a certain requirement to be met. You can only talk about a "question", if the questioner lacks knowledge and wants to remedy this deficiency through asking a "question"(cf. Seel 1983, p. 241; Zaefferer 1981, p. 46).

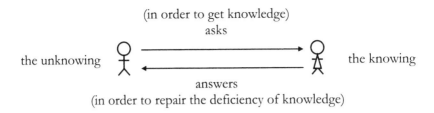

(in order to get knowledge)
asks

the unknowing — the knowing

answers
(in order to repair the deficiency of knowledge)

This kind of definition of the "question" in the scientific literature corresponds largely to our everyday understanding. Being asked by someone how to get to Berlin's radio tower, I assume that the person doesn't know the route and that exactly this ignorance is (one of) the cause(s) of their asking me the question. Of course, by asking me the questioner hopes to address the knowing person.

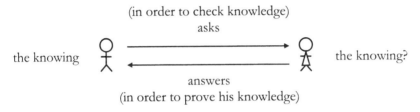

(in order to check knowledge)
asks

the knowing — the knowing?

answers
(in order to prove his knowledge)

Knowledge seeking questions: someone who lacks certain knowledge asks a knowing person about it.

Exactly at the place of teaching, however, you meet another type of question which is completely the opposite of the first one. It is commonly known as the "exam question". In his theory of speech acts J. R. Searle differentiates between "genuine questions" and "exam questions". According to him they have different communicative functions: in the case of genuine questions there is a demand for information whereas in the case of exam questions the person who has been asked has to demonstrate their knowledge (cf. Hundsnurscher 1975, p. 12). In contrast to "knowledge seeking questions" the exam questions are known as "knowing in advance questions" (cf. Holzkamp 1984, Mehan 1979). In the latter case, the person asking already possesses the information about which he asks his communication partner and can therefore decide whether the given answer is true or false. Knowing in advance questions: a knowing person who is sure of his knowledge asks his dialogue partner about knowledge of which he (the person questioned) is not certain.

The Socratic question: knowing in advance *or* knowledge seeking?

Which kind of question is dealt with in Socratic Dialogues? *Is the initial Socratic question one "with an answer known in advance"?* If this were so, then those who formulate the question and present it to the dialogue group — as a rule the facilitators — have to know the right answer to that question already. They could have a "knowledge in advance" at their disposal.

If the initial question given by the facilitator were of the kind we call "knowing in advance", then the facilitator of the Socratic Dialogue would be able to lead the group to his/her own answer to that question. Leading the group to an answer which already exists in the consciousness of the facilitator would then correspond to the teaching form called " developing by asking " which often replaces imparting knowledge in schools (cf. Loska 1995, pp. 97-131). In this case the judgement of the teacher has an indirect influence. He does not give the answers but determines, backed up by his putative knowledge, which of the given answers are true or false. Hence, this form of teaching would contradict an essential condition of the Socratic Dialogue, as formulated by Nelson:

> "The influence that may emanate from the instructor's assertions (…) must be excluded unconditionally. If this influence is not eliminated, all labour is vain. The instructor will have done everything possible to forestall the pupil's own judgement by offering him a ready-made judgement." (Nelson 1998, p. 52)

If the initial question would fall under the condition of a "knowing in advance", then it could not be the starting point of a Socratic Dialogue. But this does not neglect at all the fact that the facilitator may have previously dealt with the subject matter. Such a preparation merely helps to get an overall view of the possible methods of argument during the dialogue and especially supports his endeavour not to overlook important contributions or to enable them to get attention. Through this preoccupation with the subject matter the facilitator obtains the margin which enables him to concentrate on the dialogue process, or, as Heckmann writes "the participants begin to try to get insights and on the obstacles which have to be fought: How is one participant approaching the problem, how does it affect the other one?"(Heckmann 1993, p. 98)

It looks as though the initial question cannot be a "knowing in advance question", nor is it allowed to be one. Is the initial question a knowledge seeking question? If so, who would seek for knowledge? There are two "subjects" to choose from: the Socratic facilitator or the dialogue participants. If the facilitator looks for knowledge then the contributions of the group would be attempts to mobilise knowledge in order to repair the lack of knowledge of the facilitator as reflected by the question. The facilitator would not judge the contributions according to whether they refer to each other, whether the participants move ahead together and whether the opinions presented are mutually checked, that is, he would not do all that we normally expect from a Socratic facilitator. He would value the contributions only when considered appropriate for his subjective interest, namely obtaining knowledge.

As a rule, the Socratic facilitator cannot expect that his question will be answered directly by any participant. It looks like the participants do not have to be knowing people in order to make the Socratic question which is asked of them meaningful.

But could the participants not look for knowledge among one another, as we are acquainted with it in Socratic Dialogues? Not if the Socratic question is understood as a knowing in advance question. Through taking part in the dialogue the participants have already stated that they are *seeking* knowledge, and they do not know the answer. Therefore, as far as the answer of the question is concerned, they are not potential informants for each other either.

Summarising, we can emphasise that the initial question in the Socratic Dialogue is neither a "knowing in advance question" nor a "knowledge seeking question". It seems as if the Socratic question were a completely other kind of question than the ones mentioned above. Trying to determine the Socratic question positively seems to lead to a Socratic aporia. Neither the one nor the other way is conclusive, but we cannot do without it either.

There is a certain method of dissolving apparent aporia. It is usually introduced by a paradoxical way of thinking: Things are looked at out of wholly different perspectives and at once they suit each other although they seemed incompatible before.

The Socratic question: knowing in advance *and* seeking knowledge

The change of perspective we are here proposing consists in the withdrawal of the generalisation which had crept in above. It is not the case that every question is to be understood on the pattern of "the one who asks — the other who is asked". In the Socratic Dialogue the participants ask *themselves* about the truth of a subject matter. Together they consider which of the answers to a question (answers discovered in *themselves*) could be valid. Put roughly: Socratic questions are questions of self-knowledge: "Know thyself!" as the Delphic oracle pronounces. The duty of the facilitator is to support the dialogue group during this enterprise of acquiring *self*-knowledge.

The question in Socratic Dialogues does not only have a communicative function, but a philosophical function as well, which at the same time has didactical and methodical implications. The philosophical function is apparent in the fact that the initial question contains both components: it is both knowing in advance and knowledge seeking — but in a new sense.

Is it possible to ask about something which one already knows in advance? It is, if we consider different levels of knowledge. One can know something more or less clearly. One can be more or less sure about one's knowledge. One can share knowledge with others to different degrees. To philosophise in a Socratic manner means to try to clarify (make explicit) knowledge which has already been there in us all the time as an unclear (implicit) knowledge.

That means: the Socratic initial question is a question *knowing in advance*. It presupposes a knowledge that will be brought into the open and checked through the dialogue. The Socratic question is a *knowledge seeking* question as well. It looks for a clear and tested knowledge which still has to clarify an implicit pre-existing knowledge.

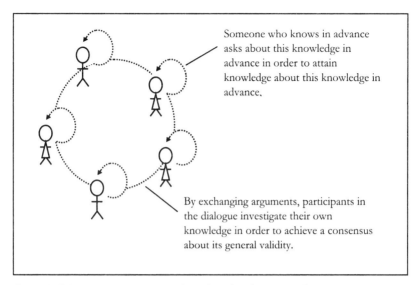

Someone who knows in advance asks about this knowledge in advance in order to attain knowledge about this knowledge in advance.

By exchanging arguments, participants in the dialogue investigate their own knowledge in order to achieve a consensus about its general validity.

Socratic initial questions must therefore be formulated in such a way that they relate to a subject matter about which there is already implicit knowledge – however clear or unclear it is – available to us. Socratic questions ask about the general characteristics of our usage of reason. If general knowledge is knowledge which can be grasped by all of the participants in a dialogue, then it is only real insight if the answer found is potentially a consensus.

2. The process of abstraction

Finally we want to deal with the process of argument and abstraction. This process seems to be the central element in SD because of the very idea of obtaining philosophical insights in answer to the Socratic question we already dealt with in chapter one. The following questions might be helpful in a systematic exploration of the process of abstraction in SD: What is abstraction, what does it mean? What do we abstract from? What is "regressive abstraction", as Leonard Nelson called the abstraction process in the Socratic dialogue? How do we come from specific judgements to abstract statements? What makes these statements valid?

What is abstraction?

In everyday language we talk about "abstract" arts, "abstract" music and "abstract" science, a term that often means somewhat "non-representational" and "hard to understand". By applying the adjective "abstract" to sciences, speeches or concepts we often suggest (a bit derogatorily) that something is "merely theoretical" and therefore "unpractical and useless in everyday life". However, in these cases "abstract" is attributed to something or is considered an attribute thereof.

Looking at the Latin origin of the word "abstract", we learn that "abstrahere" means to disregard, to ignore something. Consequently, "abstraction" is the result of an operation that starts from a more or less extensive description of a thing or a single situation, for example:

(1) I see half a billion people on the street, some of them carrying banners with the inscription "No war" on them, and others having small orange peace-buttons pinned up. → I see a demonstration for peace.

(2) That object is made of wood, has got four legs, a surface to sit on and a backrest. → This is a chair.

In these cases the step from the former to the latter statement leads to a more general concept, which covers a whole range of things or situations, ignoring details of the specific thing or concrete situation but underlining the crucial characteristics they have in common (cf. example 1 above). Finally this kind of abstraction leads to general concepts or *types*, e.g. biological species or classes of things (cf. example 2). This characterisation of "abstract" and "abstraction" approaches the philosophical meaning of the term as defined within the Aristotelian tradition. The methodological idea is to isolate aspects of something in order to gain a general insight into it.

But how would you interpret the following example?

(3) My friend Hans needed money and I have lent it to him. → In case of neediness one should help.

What is "regressive abstraction"? A theoretical explanation

Abstraction in the sense of *isolation* and *generalisation* seems to be applicable to the process of the SD too. Leonard Nelson himself described regressive abstraction in the following way: "If we inquire into the conditions of their possibility [of the judgements], we come upon more general propositions that constitute the basis of the particular judgements passed. By analysing conceded judgements we go back to their presuppositions. We operate regressively from the consequences to the reason. In this regression we eliminate the accidental facts to which the particular judgement relates and by this separation bring into relief the originally implicit assumption that lies at the bottom of the judgement on the concrete instance." (Nelson 1998, p. 48)

According to Nelson's explanation the idea of "regressive abstraction" is twofold: we have to "eliminate accidental facts" in order to bring out fully the underlying assumptions of a judgement. But this type of abstraction is embedded in a *regressive process* to the basis of the judgement, which is not reducible to the eliminatory operation. The process in question now might be understood as a special *performance of thinking and arguing*, which takes a particular experience-based judgement as its starting point. Abstraction then aims at finding an 'abstract' statement replying to a philosophical question. To gain a deeper theoretical understanding of regressive abstraction we should work out the *starting point* and the *regressive* character of argumentation in an SD. For this purpose (1) we give a broader description of the Socratic process guided by the so-called sandglass model of SD and (2) we reduce the very idea of such argumentation to its transcendental structure.

(1) The elements and structure of SD can be illustrated in the sandglass model (Kessel 2001, p. 205). Given a general question, we scrutinise a particular, practical experience and one or more related concrete judgements. Usually these judgements are the personal, more or less spontaneous and not thoroughly reflected upon opinions of the example-giver. Relying on the example and judgement we think and argue together in order to obtain, step by step, reasonable and common insights. These insights consist of various rules and values that our everyday practice, namely a decision or action, is based upon. They are formulated in 'abstract' statements, which are to be understood as the

underlying rules and conditions, or at least the basic principles, values and attitudes of our practical, experience-based judgement. Regressive abstraction thus means to move *backwards* from a concrete judgement to the initial and implicit presuppositions. By making them explicit we are trying to obtain more fundamental foundations for our judgement.

The hourglass model provides a clear and easy-to-remember view of this five-stage process. It can be used to explain the method applied in SD beforehand and it may also serve as an aid to orientation during the dialogue itself.

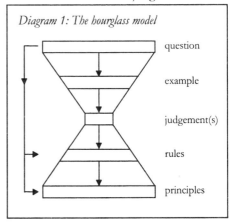

Diagram 1: The hourglass model

- question
- example
- judgement(s)
- rules
- principles

(2) Unlike isolating abstraction, regressive abstraction does not start directly from descriptions of situations and events but from *judgements about events in certain situations*. In order to grasp the basic idea of regressive abstraction, it may be most sensible to understand it as a somewhat *transcendental* argument. Nelson, being a Kantian, also seems to have had this type of argument in mind. It can be depicted in a formal question-answer sequence, which doesn't just illustrate its logical structure but also its regressive direction. As to the hourglass model, this sequence would initially start at the narrow neck ("judgement(s)") and then proceed to the base ("principles").

Formal question-answer sequence:

1. Judgement: In the face of situation S the concrete experience-based judgement J implies that p (a decision or action is right, etc.).
2. *Question:* What conditions or rules is the experience-based judgement J in S based on?
   Answer: In S, the experience-based judgement J, implying that p, is based on the rule R_s.
   In other words: J is the result of a correct

Example-dialogue:

1. At the gate to Heaven I ask St. Peter to let me in. He asks whether I have done anything good in my life. "Sure!" I reply, "for example, recently I lent Hans 400 Euro which he needed urgently. Actually I had saved the money for my vacation."
2. *St. Peter:* "Well done! But let's look at it more carefully: Why do you think it was good to lend Hans money?" *Me:* "Considering the bad situation of

application of R_s, in S.

3. *Question:* Is there any principle (or a value), which supports – the application of – R_s in S?
   Answer: The principle P (the value V) supports – the application of – R_s, as an appropriate/correct rule.
   In other words: The assertion "J is the result of a correct application of R_s in S" is correct, because there is a principle P (a value V) that supports the rule R_s.

4. *In addition to that:* whoever accepts the experience-based judgement J also has to accept the principle P (the value V), since P (V) supports the rule R_s, whose correct application in S has led to J.

Hans, it was good to lend him money, because one should help friends who are in trouble."

3. *St. Peter:* "Is there any more profound reason than that one should help friends who are in trouble, even if one therefore has to waive something?"
   Me: "If it is just at the cost of your own pleasure, then you should help not only your friends but any people in trouble."

4. *St. Peter:* "Since we are of the opinion that it was well done by you to lend Hans money, we also have to say that the imperative of helping in case of trouble is fundamentally prior to one's own pleasure."

If in this sequence the initial concrete situation S is taken into consideration all the way to the end, a connection to personal experience is equally maintained throughout the process. This important aspect of regressive abstraction is also confirmed in the very structure of the formal sequence, which can be used as a structural framework for the *reconstruction* of basic principles based on experience.

Considering that in an actual SD the judgement ought to be given a certain (possibly positive) validity during the discussion rather than just being hypothetical, i.e. that all the participants assign a certain valence (which in SD should meet the approval of all participants, if possible) to this judgement, the initial question "what makes these abstract statements valid?" turns out to be rather problematic: the catch here lies in the fact that the valence of the initial experience-based judgement remains untested within the formal regressive sequence and that the valence of the principle is related to the valence of the experiential judgement merely by arguments obtained through regressive abstraction. Nelson was well aware of this problem. To clear up the status of the results of regressive abstraction (which is only based on presumptions), he asks – considering the unsubstantiated starting point – "What should we do, then, if these data [(1) in the sequence; the authors] become doubtful? In terms of validity, they depend on and result from the principles. But it is the principles, it's their legitimacy that is disputed." (Nelson 1970, pp. 19 f.; translated by the authors) Although the connection to personal experience is provided by means of regressive abstraction, the result of this abstraction does not necessarily have to be valid.

Nelson did propose a solution to this problem. According to him, this striving for knowledge should not aim at substantiated judgements (a justified assertion) but at immediate knowledge, which — as a psychological fact — stands above the possible shortcomings of this search for reasons, and of discursive thought in general (cf. Nelson 1970, pp. 23 f.; Nelson 1973, pp. 459-483). But his suggestion reduces the discourse itself to a merely propaedeutic means of discovery. We do not consider this an acceptable solution and will instead advocate another one below.

How can the process of regressive abstraction in practical discourse be explained?

Leaving behind these abstract considerations, which were nevertheless necessary to understand the theoretical dimension of regressive abstraction, we will now focus and reflect on the practical side of an SD. It seems to be essential for those who are or would like to become Socratic facilitators to understand and analyse real discussions from the viewpoint of regressive abstraction. Being able to do so is considered to be a key prerequisite for leading a Socratic dialogue. The participants may also find it helpful to look back upon the discussion process at the end of their dialogue — for instance in form of an analytic discussion — and, if necessary, clear up possible inconsistencies and uncertainties.

Every SD that employs regressive abstraction undoubtedly demands some prior knowledge of this particular process. However, the more fiercely this knowledge is expressed, the more often it may happen that an actual SD does not really "match up" with the theory. Sometimes there is not enough time for an SD to go far enough, or the group focuses more on phenomena than on arguments, so that the example phase (search, selection and formulation of personal experiences) is given priority over other matters in this context. It may also be difficult to articulate a clear, concrete judgement. In such cases there probably won't be any (adequate) material for an analysis later on. But even if there is sufficient material, the systematic structure is rarely unambiguous, and a possible regressive argument hardly ever meets the eye immediately. There could be several strings of argumentation at different levels of abstraction, various lines of discussion, some of which are dropped at one time only to be picked up again later on. In view of the complex nature of an actual SD, the subsequent analysis should therefore be used to gain an insight into the logical sequence of the dialogue rather than forcing it into a logical outward structure.

We would now like to introduce three different ways to get a training group onto the process of regressive abstraction, all of which are appropriate to the Socratic method, i.e. founded on personal experience. The last variant will be discussed in detail.

(1) One group can look at individual discussion sequences or stages from various documented dialogues and try to find out what kind of abstraction is used in each case. Ideally, the participants in such an analytic discussion should work closely together for several sessions, they should have extensive, hands-on experience in Socratic dialogue and know how to select and examine the available "material". The person who chooses the example questions – usually the one who conducts the workshop – may also determine the kind and variety of the abstractions that need to be "spotted". In this variant, the facilitator's prior knowledge of (regressive) abstraction will have a strong influence on the group's work.

(2) With the help of the facilitator, the group can also focus right away on regressive abstraction and find out whether and how it was used in an entire, finished dialogue. This could be done in two different ways:

(2a) It certainly makes more sense if the members of the group who analyse the dialogue are also the ones who initially participated in it. Unfortunately, this approach is rather time-consuming and risky: Experience shows that it takes a very long time for discussions to reach the stage of abstraction, and very few of them even touch upon principles. Besides that, there is no guarantee that an SD really has a successful outcome and provides suitable material for an analysis.

(2b) If there is not enough time or the risk of not getting the right material for an analysis is too high, the analysis can also be based on the discussion report. One possible way to do so will be illustrated below.

Regressive abstraction in practice: an example case

The SD outlined below was part of a university seminar in environmental sociology at the University of Vienna (in 2001). Besides theories of risk, risk society and technology studies, the basic ideas of sustainable development were addressed in the course. The SD was intended to give the students the chance to improve their cognitive capacity to argue by building up — systematically and step by step — an argumentation on the issues at stake. In addition to that, the SD was presented as a method of investigating the ethical implications of sustainable development with philosophical laypersons, i.e. people who do not have specialised philosophical training or hold an academic degree in philosophy. Six students and the Socratic facilitator participated in the dialogue. The SD lasted a total of nine hours (three sessions at three hours each). None of the participants had taken part in an SD before. The question the students chose was: *"Under what circumstances does individual benefit justify collective risk?"* As usual, the dialogue started with personal examples from the participants' own experience. Paul's example was selected for two main reasons: the clarity and the comprehensiveness of the situation. Thus, all participants could easily imagine the situation of the example-giver.

SD protocol: Under what circumstances does individual benefit justify collective risk?

Paul's example in full: It was a cold day yesterday. I took my son J. to the car, which was parked five minutes walking distance from home. We picked up my wife and my other son L. from our house. L. suffers from a minor illness in his respiratory tract, which makes it advisable to prevent him from catching a cold. We drove about 500 meters to the kindergarten. After we had dropped off our children at the kindergarten, my wife and I went another 700 meters to the parking lot and took the public train to commute to work. By doing so I saved about 15 minutes (as compared to walking).

The example giver concluded his outline with a judgement: Although I am aware of the fact that driving short distances with the car is ecologically harmful, I think that my 'short-distance shuttle service' is justified because

a) otherwise I use public transport;
b) a lot of time and co-ordination are needed, and time-saving relieves parents;
c) with two small children it is easier to go by car than to walk with them;
d) I wanted to prevent my children from catching a cold.

The participants selected various individual benefits on the one hand, and collective risk on the other:

individual benefit	collective risk
comfort, saving time, preventing from catching a cold	air pollution

The group offered a range of questions and decided to concentrate on the following:

■ Does the comfort which Paul gained from his behaviour, according to judgement (b) and (c), justify the resulting air pollution?

Marie: Comfort justifies the air pollution caused by Paul driving his car only under certain circumstances (e.g. very cold, or 'real' and violating stress).

Paul: Comfort justifies using my car up to a certain threshold of the already existing air pollution.

Marie: The damage resulting from the use of the car in this situation is too big to justify the comfort.

At the end of the session the group sums up – two different positions are elaborated:

Position A: Marie, as a representative of this first position, looks upon the question from a strictly environmental point of view. Avoiding environmental damage is valued very highly from this perspective. In principle, individual behaviour ought to be aimed at reaching this goal. Only in a few exceptional cases can environmental damage be accepted.

Position B: Paul is a representative of the second position, which approaches the question from the viewpoint of individual benefit: Achieving individual benefit (comfort, health, saving time) is justified in principle; it should only be limited if the resulting environmental pollution goes beyond a certain level.

These two positions were also presented in a follow-up session focussing on the issue of health. (Interestingly, position A was defended by the non-parent members of the group, position B by parents.) In this session the dialogue moved on to the following question:

- Does the children's health according to judgement (d) justify the resulting air pollution?

Marie: The children's health justifies air pollution only in exceptional cases, e.g. if the weather is in fact very cold and if there is a high degree of probability that the child will catch a cold.

Herbert: The children's health does not justify the use of the car, since driving a car is not good for one's health either, both in the short and in the long run.

Towards the end of the session Paul suggested that there was a difference between an 'acute risk' and a 'mere creeping risk'. This differentiation led him to the following statement:

Paul: Acute risk to the children's health justifies my car drive.

Finally he contrived to articulate a viewpoint that somewhat met with general approval:

- Acute risk to someone's health justifies an individual act that entails a creeping collective risk like air pollution caused by driving a car.

Two possible exercises

Let's assume that this kind of dialogue will have to be analysed by a training group from the point of view of regressive abstraction. How can this be done?

1. Open exercise

In a very open type of exercise the group asks the following questions about the example dialogue that needs to be analysed:

- What steps of abstraction do we find in the report?
- From what do the statements abstract?
- In what way do the statements abstract?

This kind of exercise was carried out at the Birmingham Workshop on Socratic Methodology. In this case, the group found a number of different abstractions at different stages of the example dialogue:

(1) from very specific facts in the example to more general descriptions in the judgement;

(2) from facts in the example to their interpretation (meaning and evaluation) in the judgement;

(3) from statements on a personal level ("driving a car", "comfort", "individual benefit") to statements on a collective level ("air pollution", "environmental damage", "to avoid environmental damage");

(4) from specific judgements to basic reasons/rules and to principles.

However, characterising or even getting an idea of these steps of abstraction might turn out to be rather difficult. In our case the group agreed that the abstraction types (1) and (2) are not part of the process of regressive abstraction in its core meaning. Nevertheless, they are of some significance in the example phase and in formulating a concrete judgement. Finally, the group raised some important questions, which led to deeper analysis, for example:

- "What is the difference between a 'general' and a 'universal' judgement?"
- "What is the meaning and function of 'consensus' in the process of abstraction?"

Both questions are closely related. They can be used to clarify further the idea of regressive abstraction. If a judgement is considered 'general' — as opposed to 'specific' — one may assume that this judgement does not only apply to the example situation but also to many other (similar) situations. In terms of rules, one could say that a 'general rule' is applicable to a certain *type* of situation. Taking into account that there can be different degrees of 'general', i.e. that some judgements can be more or less 'general' than others, we will now be able to reconstruct *one* aspect of the regressive argumentation process: argumentation — according to the regressive structure discussed above— goes back step by step towards more 'general' judgements until it reaches the generalisation level of the Socratic question. So much for the first part of this idea.

The assertion that a judgement is 'universal', on the other hand, refers to its *validity*. A judgement can be deemed 'universal' regardless of whether it is 'general' or 'specific': even highly specific judgements[1] may have a universal claim. To determine if this claim is justified, we first have to reach a factual consensus in the SD on how the judgement is to be understood and then examine the reasons for that, i.e. find out why it is justified (e.g. on account of certain rules). In a second step, the aforementioned 'consensus' will have a *licensing function*. A *factual agreement on the validity* of a reason, which was obtained in the SD, provides us — until it is revoked — with the licence to take this reason for granted for the rest of the discussion. Thus the licensing function of a factual

---

1 As for instance in the 'general' form: "In *this* specific situation, which had the characteristics E_{1-n}, it was right to do x!"

consensus also supports what is considered to be a *constitutive element* of SD: the *claim* that *all* the participants should have the chance to gain empirical, valid insights.

Yet at this point we are facing the same problem as Nelson, who had already raised the question of whether and to what extent the result of an abstraction could be valid. It is obvious that a factual consensus cannot guarantee absolute validity. But instead of *suspending* the idea of critical examination in favour of immediate knowledge and thus decreasing the significance of discussion, we should first *mentally expand* it beyond the existing temporal and personal dimensions of a factual SD. In fact, we have to imagine a limitless SD where possible objections will have to be justified in the face of a *now* factually derived consensus. This by no means refutes the idea of discussion but rather proposes it as the only sensible way to counteract a lack of appropriate reasons *in the long run*. "Consent", again, is necessary in order to be able to narrow the entire range of possible reasons down to a single one that can be freely accepted by all. After all, it also has the function of a *regulative idea* (Kant).

Nonetheless, although absolutely valid insights may be gained *in the long run*, most of the time they don't seem to be available *now*. But is this really the case? Could this also be true for the constitutive claim of the SD? A training group and/or SD group can investigate this by means of a *reflexive dialogic test*, which uses a current situation as a starting point rather than a past experience. In this case, one participant asks himself/herself: "As a participant in an SD, can I say without being contradicted: 'I assume that there are no valid insights whatsoever?'" This will definitely make it clear that in this example the participant's doubts about how his/her question will be received make no sense, because with the *act* of assuming something "I" already take for a fact that what "I" assume — i.e. the general doubt — *is* already an insight. In other words: everybody needs to agree beforehand that valid insights can be gained in an SD *(a priori consensus)*.

2.   Analysis based on Toulmin's model of argument

Stephen Toulmin, in *The Uses of Argument* (1958, pp. 94 ff., esp. pp. 101 ff.), has developed an analysis of argument which can be applied in particular to practical discourse and which makes it a lot easier to structure discussions and recognise inferences.

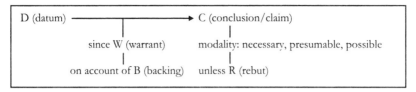

A rough comparison of the different steps in the hourglass model and the main aspects of the argumentation scheme shows that both models use elements with essentially the same functions:

hourglasss model	*elements of the argumentation scheme*
question	–
example	datum
judgement	conclusion (claim)
rules	since W (warrant)
principles	on account of B (backing)

As opposed to the more or less detailed description of an experienced situation in a real SD, Toulmin's scheme only concentrates on the facts that are relevant for the judgement ("datum"). They can be understood as the result of an *isolating* abstraction, since the details and circumstances which have — even though they are part of the experience — no influence on the judgement are *left aside*. In an SD, these facts can be obtained without any major circumlocution by following the five steps for documenting the example (cf. Kopfwerk 2004, p. 163).

Toulmin's scheme, to be used as an heuristic tool, seems to be better suited to analyse a dialogue than the hourglass model, as it also takes into account a variety of modes and exceptional conditions and is therefore more sensitive to the detailed structure of individual arguments.

Let us now take a closer look at the dialogue report and especially at the question "Under what circumstances does individual benefit justify collective risk?" Including the *prima facie* reasons (a) to (d), the example-giver's judgement with regard to his behaviour was quite elaborate. The group then decided to start with the benefit of comfort and timesaving in this context, and then to proceed with the health issue. During the dialogue the group split up into two camps: one following a more ecological line of argumentation (position A), the other following a more pragmatic line, focussing more on human aspects (position B). Despite the different starting points both positions acknowledged the necessity of environmental protection on the one hand and the consideration of pragmatic constraints on the other hand. Unfortunately, the degree of admissible environmental damage and/or the constraints of everyday life could not be discussed any further. In a final step, the different lines of argumentation were also applied to the other examples given at the beginning of the seminar.

Toulmin's scheme can be effectively used by a training group to decode individual arguments. If we select position B, for instance, which is also the example-giver's position, and fit it into the structure of the scheme, we may arrive at the following picture (with the respective inferences highlighted):

Diagram 1: Position B

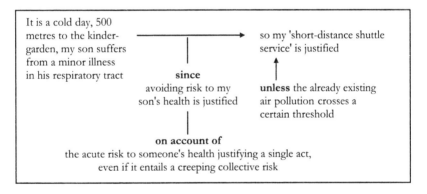

Double structure model of regressive abstraction

For a better understanding of the regression process that goes on during the course of our example dialogue, Toulmin's model of argument will have to be somewhat expanded. This is necessary because the narrowed-down version of this scheme makes no allowances for any kind of explanations — notwithstanding that they might be indispensable to discussion in a SD.

Diagram 2: Double structure model (position B)

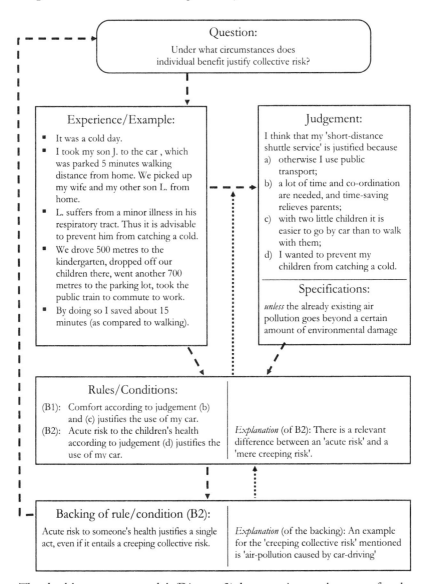

Question:

Under what circumstances does individual benefit justify collective risk?

Experience/Example:

- It was a cold day.
- I took my son J. to the car , which was parked 5 minutes walking distance from home. We picked up my wife and my other son L. from home.
- L. suffers from a minor illness in his respiratory tract. Thus it is advisable to prevent him from catching a cold.
- We drove 500 metres to the kindergarten, dropped off our children there, went another 700 metres to the parking lot, took the public train to commute to work.
- By doing so I saved about 15 minutes (as compared to walking).

Judgement:

I think that my 'short-distance shuttle service' is justified because
a) otherwise I use public transport;
b) a lot of time and co-ordination are needed, and time-saving relieves parents;
c) with two little children it is easier to go by car than to walk with them;
d) I wanted to prevent my children from catching a cold.

Specifications:

unless the already existing air pollution goes beyond a certain amount of environmental damage

Rules/Conditions:

(B1): Comfort according to judgement (b) and (c) justifies the use of my car.
(B2): Acute risk to the children's health according to judgement (d) justifies the use of my car.

Explanation (of B2): There is a relevant difference between an 'acute risk' and a 'mere creeping risk'.

Backing of rule/condition (B2):

Acute risk to someone's health justifies a single act, even if it entails a creeping collective risk.

Explanation (of the backing): An example for the 'creeping collective risk' mentioned is 'air-pollution caused by car-driving'

The double structure model *(Diagram 2)* does not just make room for the Socratic question and important explanations, it also shows that the process of regressive abstraction moves in two opposite directions: One direction (broken arrow) presents the step-by-step development of the SD, during which the participants try to find prerequisites (rules, principles and/or warrant, backing) for the validity of the judgement. In the opposite direction (dotted arrow) — in other words, going backwards from the backing of rules to the rules themselves and then to the judgement — these prerequisites now serve as a reason for the initial judgement.

How to end?

There is a very important question which came up in our workshop at the 2002 Newman Conference at Birmingham: "How to end a dialogue well?" The following answer with which we want to conclude our essay may be a good one. It consists of questions for you: What kind of knowledge have we gained? Are those insights relevant for our life and (Socratic) work? What other kinds of questions come into our minds? Are there some other important methodological aspects we should take into account? The dialogue goes on. The dialogue group of Kopfwerk Berlin warmly invites you to take part in its ongoing work on the methodology of Socratic Dialogue. Please consult us and send us your questions, suggestions, proposals and ideas: socratic-methodology@Kopfwerk-Berlin.de

Reverences

Holzkamp, Klaus (1994): Am Problem vorbei — Zusammenhangs-blindheit der Variablenpsychologie. In: Forum Kritische Psychologie 34, pp. 80-94.

Hundsnurscher, Franz (1975): Semantik der Fragen. In: Zeitschrift für germanistische Linguistik (ZGL) 3, pp. 1-14.

Gronke, Horst; Stary, Joachim (1998): Sapere aude! Das Neosokratische Gespräch als Chance für die universitäre Kommunikationskultur. In: Handbuch Hochschullehre, Informationen und Handreichungen aus der Praxis für die Hochschullehre. Loseblattsammlung. Bonn: Raabe-Verlag, 19. Ergänzungslieferung, Chap. A. 2.11, pp. 1-34.

Heinen-Tenrich, Jürgen; Horster, Detlef; Krohn, Dieter (eds.) (1989): Das Sokratische Gespräch. Ein Symposion. Hamburg: Junius.

Kessels, Jos (1997): Socrates op de markt. Filosofie in bedrijf. Boom: Meppel/Amsterdam.

Kopfwerk (2004): The Methodology of Socratic Dialogue: Creating Socratic Questions and the Importance of Being Specific. In: P. Shipley; H. Mason (eds.): Ethics and Socratic Dialogue in Civil Society. Series on Socratic Philosophizing. Vol. XI, London/Münster: Lit, pp. 148-168.

Loska, Rainer (1995): Lehren ohne Belehrung. Bad Heilbrunn: Klinkhardt.

Nelson, Leonard (1970): Die Schule der kritischen Philosophie und ihre Methode. In: Gesammelte Schriften. Vol. I, ed. by P. Bernay, W. Eichler, A. Gysin, Hamburg: Meiner.

Nelson, Leonard (1973): Geschichte und Kritik der Erkenntnistheorie. In: Gesammelte Schriften. Vol. II, ed. by P. Bernay, W. Eichler, A. Gysin, Hamburg: Meiner.

Nelson, Leonard (1998): The Socratic Method. In: P. Shipley (ed.): Occasional Working Papers in Ethics and the Critical Philosophy. Vol. 1, London: The Society for the Furtherance of the Critical Philosophy, pp. 42-62.

Schwarzbach (1985): Problem und Problemverhalten. In: Gorny, E.; Falkenhagen, H.; Knopf, H. (eds.): Theoretische und empirische Untersuchungen zum Frage- und Kontrollverhalten in der Lerntätigkeit. Halle-Wittenberg.

Searle, John Roger (1969): Speech Acts: An Essay in the Philosophy of Language. Cambridge: University Press.

Seel, Norbert M. (1983): Fragenstellen und kognitive Strukturierung. In: Psychololgie in Erziehung und Unterricht 30, pp. 241-252.

Toulmin, Stephen (1958): The Uses of Argument. Oxford University Press.

Zaefferer, Dietmar (1981): Fragesätze und andere Formulierungen von Fragen. In Krallmann, D.; Stickel, G. (eds.): Zur Theorie der Frage. Tübingen: GNV.

Gale Prawda

Business Ethics and Socratic Dialogue

Ethics in the business world is viewed from several different perspectives. This might lead us to ask: if the different perspectives yield different responses to the same ethical issue in question, which response would be considered 'ethically correct' or right? In business these days the buzzwords in this area seem to be 'responsibility', 'accountability', and so on. When an accident arises in which human life has been harmed or endangered, we ask who or what is responsible/accountable for the incident? The question of right or wrong acts comes up even in less dramatic situations in the workplace. The relativism of ethics in business is further complicated by other factors such as: cultural influences and environment, the uncertainty of ethics in a newly developed sector (what are the norms since they are derived from practice not yet experienced or in the process of being experienced?), as well as the universal approach to ethics as exemplified in the 'Human Rights' Charter (legislated and executed by the United Nations). Presently, all these variants constitute structures in which ethical choice is made.

The standard ethical systems with which we are familiar boil down to: utilitarianism, deontology, and the NORM theory ('neutral omnipartial rule making' as elaborated by Green). By taking an ethical dilemma as an example for decision making we could very easily come up with three different responses to the same conflict. Before considering these three ethical theories, it might be wise to consider a more basic question: what constitutes an ethical dilemma? One main view states that an issue is ethical when there is a conflict of interests between two or more parties in which an act is carried out by one of the parties at the expense of the other(s) concerned. This perhaps may be a very broad position and even the dynamics of this definition could not cover all grounds (for an act carried out by one party at the expense of another in response to a conflict of interests may not be considered in the ethical domain at all, but purely empirical). We also run into the cultural relativist argument, whereby the so-called 'conflict of interests' or 'conflict of values' may only be apparent to one side, or in fact, interpreted in two different perspectives, hence coming up with two different 'ethical issues'. And lastly, when the norms have not yet been established in newly developed areas (e. g. the Internet, bioethics and euthanasia) the conflicts and the values involved may be difficult to discern. In spite of these obstacles, decision making in an ethical context is a reality as well as a necessity. Those facing these dilemmas are becoming more aware of dealing with ethical issues despite the difficulties they present.

The workshop at the Loccum Conference on Business Ethics and Socratic Dialogue (N° 14) was designed to bring forward the different outcomes of the same ethical issue based upon the theory used to analyse it. The same case study was given to each group (one group represented the utilitarian approach, another group the deontological approach and lastly the NORM theory approach). Briefly summarising the case study: a fellow (doctor) colleague at a psychiatric training centre, while looking for some documents to complete his report found some letters, photos, and other incriminating evidence in his colleague's desk. He took these items to the Head of the centre and demanded immediate dismissal of his colleague. The Head of the division was faced with the question: could she use this evidence that was taken from someone's desk as grounds upon which to take action? If she did take action, what would sort of action would it be? (Green 1994, pp. 171-173).

(1) The *Utilitarian* group discussed this case based on the premise of 'the greatest good for the greatest number' in which confronting the doctor concerned and perhaps firing him on the grounds of his misconduct would keep the other stakeholders involved happy. The other stakeholders outweighed both quantitatively and qualitatively the consideration of the doctor and his family. In determining which action would produce more good than bad by weighing the total good results (in terms of happiness) against the total bad ones and by comparing the results/consequences of the various actions, the action that produces the most good is the one considered to be morally right. The psychiatric training centre, its staff, residents and others would benefit from the dismissal of the doctor due to his misconduct.

(2) The *deontological* group discussed this case on the basis of the moral rules involved, finding that the misconduct demonstrated by this

discovery of information, would call for the dismissal of the doctor in question. In other words, he broke the rules and should be responsible for his acts. If not immediate dismissal than a strong warning not to repeat this misconduct would be required. Though, in this case there were two rules in conflict: professional behaviour and privacy in the workplace. Since the incriminating material used as proof of misconduct was found in a personal area (desk), could this material be used to confront the doctor on his misconduct. Which rule is more important (prima facie) misconduct or privacy?

(3) The *NORM* ('neutral omnipartial rule-making') *theory* group, though restricted by time, would have come up with some sort of rule adapted to this situation after a thorough analysis of the stakeholders involved. Referring to Green's *The Ethical Manager* (from which the case was taken) two propositions appear:

'First Proposed Moral Rule: whenever materials in an employee's desk or files are urgently needed for the proper functioning of the organisation and when the employee (or manager) is absent from work or otherwise unable to give permission, a supervisor or fellow employee may conduct a thorough search for those materials.

Second Proposed Moral Rule: whenever a supervisor suspects an employee (or manager) of serious misconduct that disrupts the organisational functioning or violates others' rights, and when materials in the employee's desk or files might help the supervisor to determine the facts, the supervisor may, without the employee's permission or other authorisation, conduct a search to obtain these materials.' (Ibid., p. 176)

These two possible propositions are quite different in nature. The first would be considered more like a guideline type of rule in which the person in question is treated neutrally, whereas the second one grants authorisation (when a staff member is suspected of something) to search for the materials. In this NORM analysis, once the proposed moral rules are determined, a further look into them is necessary.

However, the most interesting aspect of this workshop demonstrated the obstacle of cultural relativism. All participants were from Europe and therefore the ethical issue they focused on was the misconduct of the doctor in question, not the question of 'privacy' in the workplace. As this case was drawn from an American business ethics perspective, the references to the analysis came from American norms (referring specifically to privacy acts in the constitution). Most participants didn't see an issue arising from how the materials were gathered (i. e. from someone's desk in their absence) for the desk and its contents were considered to belong to the organisation. Someone working in that organisation doesn't necessarily have a 'private zone'. The notion of privacy in this context was viewed from two different perspectives.

Once again with the time constraints of the workshop, there was a brief discussion covering business ethics and Socratic Dialogue. If the case study was used as the example, we could then derive the questions at stake, thereby deciding on which one was most apparent by a group consensus. Some possible questions could have been: 'What is misconduct?' 'When is it appropriate to take action when misconduct arises?' 'What is privacy?' 'Is there privacy in a public realm?'. For the briefness of the discussion that ensued, the value of a Socratic Dialogue would be that it could perhaps help in determining the norms and values prior to any ethical analysis. In other words, Socratic Dialogue would be an essential method prior to further investigation in order to determine what the norm/value is in and of itself (its essence). Clearing up misunderstandings of certain concepts and determining what the norm in question really means could be necessary preliminary groundwork, essential to any moral decision making.

There were two occasions at the conference that alerted my attention to potential flaws concerning the Socratic Dialogue method. The first came up during another workshop on the 'strategy' of the method. The question was on tolerance, and one participant, coming from a completely different culture and having gone through a 2 day dialogue inquiry, didn't understand tolerance in the way in which the other participants in the group understood it. This question of understanding came up at the 'strategy' workshop, as the group were inquiring into the next step, one member stated that his understanding of tolerance was completely different to those of the group and therefore couldn't decide on which direction to follow since he didn't fully comprehend tolerance in the same way. Spontaneously, it was suggested to break out of the method and to have a closer look at what tolerance meant to each participating member. This discussion clarified and elucidated the different cultural perspectives one has on the notion of tolerance. As the Socratic Dialogue is used in multicultural environments, there should be some sort of safety device to avoid culturally specific concepts being presented as universal.

The second incident of a lesser degree occurred during the workshop on business ethics and Socratic Dialogue. One participant thought that, as this was a workshop on business ethics, it would have been more appropriate to have chosen a case study that clearly brought up the conflict of interests or ethical issues around 'profit orientation'. One of the main reasons I chose a case study removed from this dilemma was to illustrate that ethical issues in a business context are not linked to 'profit orientation' only and that, in fact, ethics in this context is a much broader domain. However, it was mentioned that depending upon the socio-politico-economic and cultural model used, ethical evaluations would be somewhat determined by the specific models used. Can Socratic dialogue help us to go beyond these models ?

References

Green, Ronald M. (1994): The Ethical Manager. A New Method for Business Ethics. Englewood Cliffs: Macmillan.

Patricia Shipley/Fernando Leal

The Perils of Practice: A Critical View of the Practical Turn in Contemporary Philosophy[1]

"Wealth is like sea-water; the more we have, the thirstier we become; and the same is true of fame."   (Schopenhauer 1851, Parerga and Paralipomena i. 347)

In this paper we critically review the growth of philosophy in the market-place in late modernity and ask whether practical philosophy is for private profit or for the public good. Two main forms of such practice are identified here: the practice of Neo-Socratic Dialogue in small groups in organisations, and one-to-one philosophical counselling of individual 'clients'. The relevance of professionalism for commercialised applied philosophy is discussed. This paper goes on to emphasise the importance of ethics for philosophy in practice. Psychology is the discipline which is most related to practical philosophy and it is growing in ethical awareness and in ethical practice. We suggest that co-operation between the two disciplines could be to mutual advantage. Philosophical counsellors, for example, may be at risk of engaging with vulnerable individuals who are in need of protection from practitioners who are not trained to deal with their problems. We conclude that private practice does not have to be incompatible with the public good. We also conclude, however, that there is a pressing need for eternal vigilance by practitioners from such disciplines whether professionalised or not, in the complex modern 'runaway world'.

"As Education officer of the British Humanist Association I am often asked to represent a non-religious ethical perspective at conferences for sixth-formers. (…) I can't help feeling that professional philosophers might do it better than we can, if only they would come out of their

---

1   We are grateful for the support of the Society for the Furtherance of the Critical Philosophy, London, in the preparation of this paper. Some of the views expressed herein are not necessarily held by other members of the SFCP.

117

university seminar rooms and try to communicate clearly and accessibly with non-specialists. (…) It would be good to see more philosophers actively involved in committees, quangos, the media, politics, moving discussions about ethical issues onto a more rational basis, representing those of us who care about moral issues but don't feel adequately represented by a bishop or rabbi. One place to start this revolution would be in schools. University philosophy departments have often been dismissive about philosophy in schools …" (Marilyn Mason 2000, p.8)

"Into the crowded space of Periclean Athens came the wandering teachers, selling their wisdom to the bewildered populace. Any charlatan could make a killing, if enough people believed in him. Men like Gorgias and Protagoras, who wandered from house to house demanding fees for their instruction, preyed on the gullibility of a people made anxious by war. To the young Plato, who observed their antics with outrage, these 'sophists' were a threat to the very soul of Athens. One alone among them seemed worthy of attention, and that one, the great Socrates who Plato immortalised in his dialogues, was not a sophist, but a true philosopher.
The philosopher, in Plato's characterisation, awakens the spirit of enquiry (…) and his duty is to help us to be what we are — free and rational beings (…). The sophists are back with a vengeance, and are all the more to be feared, in that they come disguised as philosophers. For, in this time of helpless relativism and subjectivity, philosophy alone has stood against the tide, reminding us that those crucial distinctions on which life depends — between true and false, good and evil, right and wrong — are objective and binding." (Roger Scruton 1997)

The complete story of philosophy as a professional occupation remains yet to be told. Philosophy in Europe continued to be monopolised for centuries after the classical era by gentlemen of means and leisure. These were 'the early moderns'. There is an interesting distinction — a tension — in contemporary philosophy, however. We can write or talk about philosophy or actually 'practise' it as a trade. We are witnessing a new phenomenon — the growth of applied, practical or professional philosophy; the doing of philosophy in the 'real world'. With so many 'early modern' philosophers for so long confined to cloister and ivory tower or coffee club and occupied with writing or talking about philosophy it appears that philosophy is becoming more 'down to earth', more practical.

With notable exceptions philosophers have for some time adopted a seemingly indifferent attitude to getting involved as philosophers in real world problems, maintaining a lofty, aloof and other-worldly distance from them, and from ordinary people. Ordinary people today, on the other hand, are seriously looking for meaning in their lives and many have explored New Age 'solutions'. Some are now beginning to turn to the new philosopher guru for help.

Specifically, in the last couple of centuries philosophy has confined itself mainly to academia, and practical philosophy applied outside academia has been an occasional voluntary activity for individual academics. But it is different now. Many more philosophers are 'getting their hands dirty' in the messy outside world. Contemporary practical philosophy can take one of two general forms. It can be a voluntary, non-commercial, non-profit-making activity, or be used for commercial purposes. There is, for example, a growth in popular philosophy, such as the 'Philosophy for All' movement in London, where anyone interested, not just trained philosophers, meets to discuss philosophy in cafes and other public spaces and on country walks. The French call this activity 'café philosophique'. For the British it is 'pub philosophy'. This kind of activity is usually under the guidance of trained philosophers, some of whom are based in academic departments of philosophy.

As an extra-mural activity academy-based philosophers are from time to time invited by the authorities to sit on ethics boards and committees, and they occasionally contribute to media discussions on ethical and other issues. British television, for example, has for a few years now sought to popularise philosophy and a recent television drama featured a fictitious philosophy graduate working as an ethical consultant alongside members of health care teams in a Scottish hospital. This could be called 'media philosophy'. Julian Baggini names all this contemporary practical philosophy 'fringe' philosophy. He sees it as an identifiable movement outside the academy, and as becoming "the public face of philosophy". For him, "applied ethics is indeed the field where academia and the fringe meet." (Julian Baggini, 1999, pp. 11-12)

Ethics was a central pillar of philosophy for the Ancients, and then ethics was lost to us for many years, only making a comeback in Britain in the latter half of the twentieth century.

The main interest of our paper is centred on those applied and practical philosophers who are seeking to earn their living primarily in the exercise of philosophy as a trade, and who are not predominantly the academic teachers of the discipline. The philosophical fare on sale in the free market at present takes two main forms: there is a form of Neo-Socratic Dialogue (SD) in small groups, and 'philosophical counselling' (PC) on the one-to-one model. A growing number of philosophers are entering the market-place and, 'media philosophy' apart, SD and PC are the main goods and services on offer by these practitioners. And who should blame these business-minded philosophers in our enterprising modern world of late capitalism with its highly competitive commerce and restless consumption, and the search for 'personal growth' and self-development among the growing middle classes?

In fact, only a few years ago, the British Prime Minister berated the academic departments of philosophy in her country for what she regarded as their comparative uselessness. In 1983 her Secretary of State for Education decreed that a philosophy graduate was not eligible to teach. The immediate effect of this pronouncement was the closure of seven UK academic departments of philosophy and job losses for philosophers. Where else should displaced faculty members then go with their philosophical expertise except to the market-place, which could, in any case, one might think, well do with some outside help in attaining clarity of thought and 'mission'? (We have not forgotten that some applied philosophers will have chosen to apply their special skills anyway in the outside world of business and commerce for other reasons, and not because they found themselves out of a job in schools or the academy.)

What, however, the implications of this new trend in philosophy are for the reputation and integrity of philosophy and for the well-being of the recipients of her commercialised products and services invites our consideration. But before further deliberation we think some history should be introduced, starting briefly with the Philosophical Counselling (PC) movement and then moving on to talk in a little more detail about modern Socratic Dialogue (SD).

Philosophical Counselling

The history of PC is more recent than that of SD. The German philosopher, Gerd Achenbach is usually cited as the founder of PC, in Cologne in 1982. The aims of PC are less than clear. In particular, is it, or is it not, some kind of therapy? The use of language, its nomenclature, is important and symbolic for the image of PC. One popular UK philosophy magazine, for example, ran a regular feature by a counselling philosopher, who is also trained in psychotherapy, and the feature was called 'The Clinic' which, of course, is suggestive of psychotherapy.[2] When talking informally to PC practitioners — those who make a living out of 'counselling' — the stock response we have encountered is that 'it is not psychotherapy'; that it does not deal with the typical concerns of

---

2   Tim LeBon; The Clinic. The Philosophers' Magazine, 10, 2000 p. 27. This one example taken from the series is about 'the good life'. In an article ('What do philosophical practitioners do?') as part of the special Forum: 'Philosophy, Psychiatry and Counselling', The Philosophers' Magazine 3, 36, 1998, Jeremy Stangroom qualifies the view held by some practitioners that the future for practical philosophers is bright. "The relationship between a nascent philosophical counselling and the established mental health disciplines has yet to be worked through. The stakes are high, certainly in the States, where healthcare is big business". In the next article in the Forum, on the other hand, Lou Marinoff expresses the view that "The professionalization of philosophy in America is well underway". So, which view is more realistic?
In contrast, Margaret Goord's article in the same Forum ('Philosophical Practice: the case against') is more critical of PC practice. Her article is also refreshingly non-vituperative, and free of attack on psychologists. She cites the view expressed by the former president of the American Psychological Association that "philosophical counsellors naively assume that purely intellectual discourse can address problems that are intractably emotional and sometimes severely debilitating". (The New York Times, 8, 3, 1998)
Clearly, the debate is more advanced in the States than elsewhere, though a report of a workshop discussing the future of PC, held in London in 1996, (Philosophy Today, 24, 9) concluded that a more modest posture over PC was to be recommended to philosophers who are not renowned for the interpersonal skills needed for the counselling role, that particular skills and a body of knowledge available in psychotherapy, psychiatry and counselling would be not only useful but perhaps also necessary, and that philosophical counsellors "should confine themselves to the simplest issues, such as using Socratic Dialogue with counsellees who are not in the position of needing clinical psychotherapy".

the psychotherapist, such as with the sub-conscious mind or with destructive emotions.

That may be so but earlier, an American, James Elliott, founder of the US Institute for Clinical Philosophy, who claims to have coined the term 'clinical philosophy' in 1973, argued that his particular brand is a kind of integration of philosophy and psychotherapy. A Dutchman, Cyril Vink, regards himself as pioneer of philosophy as therapy. The French have 'La philosophie dans le cabinet', and issues tackled, it is said, are not Freudian but existential: they are about la mort, l'amour, le véritable sens de la vie, and les problèmes quotidiens des humains. We will return to the topic of PC later after a brief look at the history of modern SD and the contemporary SD scene.

Some History about Socratic Dialogue

As we all know, philosophical dialogue as a general method in philosophy has a very long history. We do not intend to rehearse the now well-known story about Socrates and the Platonic Dialogues. We want, instead, to consider briefly here the work of the little-known Göttingen University teacher of philosophy, the Kantian Leonard Nelson (1882-1927) who initiated his own version of SD. Disgusted with the inefficiencies and corruption of the Weimar Republic and deeply concerned about rising fascism in his own country Nelson founded a political party within the German socialist and working class movements of the time. He also founded a Philosophical Political Academy (PPA) for adults and a special school for children.

Nelson single-mindedly and disinterestedly dedicated all his energy, time and financial resources to the cause of ethics in politics, education and scholarship. This is a completely different picture of what an ethical life can be from anything to be observed in philosophers, and more generally intellectuals, of his time (or indeed of ours). With the possible exception of people like Max Weber and Otto Neurath most of them scarcely did more than put in an occasional appearance when a fashionable matter came up in public (see the Dreyfus affair). And even when they spoke publicly, they very often explicitly denied that they were defending anything but their own personal opinions (Bertrand Russell, for example).

For Nelson, on the other hand, the cause of ethics was never a matter of mere opinion, but of philosophy as carefully and rationally thought through and argued for as it was carefully and energetically put into practice. A few years after his early death, many of Nelson's students who had become his disciples risked life and limb as members of the German resistance movement in their struggle against the Nazis. Many were imprisoned or sent to camps and others had to disperse as refugees around the world, some ending up in London to found the Society for the Furtherance of the Critical Philosophy (SFCP). The small band of disciples — they called themselves 'ethical socialists' — lived quite frugal lives in keeping with Nelsonian ethics, making many personal sacrifices.

This small group of Nelsonians is probably one of the few modern examples (if indeed not the only one) of putting philosophy truly into practice. They did not just argue and talk about philosophy, they actually lived it in a fully committed way; indeed as a way of life. Perhaps they are a 20th century model of what those Ancient Greeks meant by philosophy. The Parisian classicist, Pierre Hadot, reminds us that philosophy was fundamentally 'a way of life' for the Ancients, not just a job (Hadot 1995). It was an ancient tradition that demanded regular and disciplined engagement in solitary 'spiritual exercises' and reflective meditations, as well as dialogues. The aim of these exercises was to achieve an inner transformation of the self, of one's whole being, leading to a 'lived ethics' — a self-consciously rational moral life. The Ancients' entire lives were to reflect their convictions. They also wanted to try and change the world for the better. This ancient concept — of 'philosophy as a way of life' — had eventually all but disappeared in a modern world in which philosophy became an academic institution of the state.

In the first part of the 20th century Nelson revived and changed the ancient method of SD, as a pedagogic and ethical tool. He preferred to teach philosophy by 'philosophising' and this was to be primarily by means of his own form of SD, the centrepiece of his German Academy. He also aimed to build character and develop ethical consciousness and was passionately committed to the putting of Kantian ethics into practice. He developed a Socratic Dialogue (the 'Nelson-Heckmann Socratic Dialogue') which is distinct in a number of ways from the classical method, and his followers have gone on to make refinements to it, especially Gustav Heckmann after the second world war.

Nelson changed the structure of the dialogues, for example, so that a circle of people could reason things out together under the guidance of a trained facilitator. After the war, his disciple Heckmann went on to develop rules for the dialogues and introduced the 'metadialogue' — a kind of dialogue on the dialogue as an integral part of the dialogue process.

Contemporary Socratic Dialogue and the Leusden-Loccum Debate

"Even when the topic is not about ethics or does not use ethical language, the practice of Socratic Dialogue is inherently ethical because it requires respect for others expressed as listening and responding to what others have said, taking responsibility for one's own contributions, reflecting on one's own role, and a painstaking co-operative approach to pursuing the truth through consensus. This demands virtue and establishes equality amongst participants.

These ethical elements in Socratic Dialogue are the core that must be preserved even as variations and adaptations of the format are developed for use in a variety of contexts." (Van Hooft 2000, pp. 75-77)

Our paper arose mainly out of our deliberations following the 2nd International Conference in Leusden, Holland in 1998 on 'The Dutch Experience', and the 3rd International Conference on 'Ethics and the Socratic Dialogue' held in Loccum, Germany in July 2000. The Leusden event informally raised many issues of practical ethical significance about the use of Socratic Dialogue in the market-place, which the Loccum conference was subsequently set up to address more explicitly and formally. Whilst we welcomed the airing in public of many of these issues at Loccum we were left with a strong feeling of 'unfinished business' and this paper is intended to keep the debate alive.

That we have not been alone in our feelings is suggested by Van Hooft's judgement following the above quoted statement from the Loccum event which in his view "fails to address the central question, namely: does Socratic Dialogue, by virtue of its critical and rational method, uncover objective, normative, and emancipatory truths when conducted in a context of pure philosophical inquiry, and would such a goal be compromised if Socratic Dialogues were conducted in contexts burdened by the necessity to make practical decisions?" (ibid, pp. 76-77)

The traditional method for training Socratic facilitators has three stages: firsthand experience as a dialogue participant, observing and reporting on dialogues under supervision, followed by supervised facilitation as a trainee. For a more detailed description of the Nelson-Heckmann method see Birnbacher who described the potential use of the method for the teaching of medical ethics (cf. Birnbacher 1999, pp. 219-224). German Socratics help to train school teachers in the method in Germany where 'practical philosophy' and ethics are a part of the regular curriculum.

The 'Society for Socratic Facilitators' in Germany now has over thirty members, all of whom are trained in the Nelson-Heckmann method, and who have in the main tended to follow a cultural norm in the spirit of the founder of not charging fees for their services. The founder had never to our knowledge envisaged his method as a commercial tool. For him its sole purposes were pedagogical, and political, i.e. in the service of left wing politics. In general among the 'German Socratics' today small Socratic groups are facilitated in holiday course settings and at conferences on a non-profit basis. The groups are intended for ordinary people who do not need to be trained in philosophy. Nelson himself came from a comparatively comfortable family and his personal Chair at Göttingen was unsalaried. His disciples were expected by him to live frugal ethical personal lives in the service of their own community and of ethical socialism.

Eventually, individuals from other countries found their way to Germany for experience in the method and for training in its facilitation. Some have gone on to initiate the method in their own country. The 'Dutch Socratics' were the first to take advantage and several Dutch facilitators have introduced the method into Dutch organisations. A pioneer is Jos Kessels, who describes in his book the application of abbreviated versions of the method in organizations.[3] Kessels takes the view that it is acceptable to use SD in business in the way that Socrates

---

3   This controversial application of the Nelson-Heckmann method is described by the Dutch philosopher Jos Kessels 1997. The book is also published in German.

also practised his philosophy in the market-place; Plato and Socrates quite explicitly intended philosophy to be used in practice.

Debates among the German and Dutch Socratics refer to 'pure' and less pure forms of Nelson-Heckmann dialogue and to 'long' and 'short' versions. These roughly correspond respectively to the traditional German and the pragmatic Dutch approaches. The one is the more Platonic and reflective of axiological or value rationality — to use Weber's terms. The other is more reminiscent of Weber's instrumental rationality, of technocracy and management consultancy. The underlying issue is the use to which the dialogues are put: whose interests they might be serving. See also our recent joint paper elaborating the theme of ethics, value conflicts and multiple mandates in professions.[4]

Well, Plato is quite clear that the followers of Socrates, who was a humble stonemason by trade, 'kept' him when he gave up his trade to philosophise and became as poor as a church mouse. The Sophists became rich from what they charged for their services but Socrates never became rich.

The commercialisation of the Nelsonian SD has inevitably led to tensions and controversy within the modern SD fraternity. Some German Socratics object to this seeming exploitation of the method, believing it is an abuse of the founder's intentions. Not all the Dutch Socratics take fees from use of the method, however, and some of the Dutch applications of SD are in the public sector, not only in private organisations. Some are no doubt voluntary and unpaid as happens also in Britain. German Socratics may also take fees from time to time when applying the method, although the voluntary tradition is much stronger there. In fact, all people employed as philosophers today take fees of one

---

4   Leal & Shipley 2002, pp. 139-161. In our joint paper to this APROS (2000) conference in Sydney last December we explored the idea of the conflicts of interest and 'dual mandates' hidden in many so-called 'good jobs', within the framework of a discussion about modern job types, value conflicts and ethics, and informed by Weber's theory of rationality. Professional jobs we suggest are typically 'dual mandate' jobs when they become part of institutions. Whose interests do they really serve? For example, does the factory medical physician put the interests of the individual patient qua worker first or the interests of the firm when these clash? Philosophers who act as management consultants may find themselves torn between, say, promoting the profit side of business or its social responsibility, bearing in mind that one particularly powerful alternate view is that the business of business is business and not social responsibility which is the business of government.

kind or another, either from the state as teachers of philosophy, or from private sources.

Whither Practical Philosophy? The Institutionalisation of Psychology and Philosophy

Commercialised philosophical counselling has become an international movement and there is also the prospect that modern versions of SD may soon catch up with it in the market-place. Who knows in these enterprising days what other practical and commercially viable techniques in philosophy will then be invented? It seems tardy, therefore, to ask whether philosophy should be offered in the market-place at all. Despite the supposed honourable philosophical tradition of keeping philosophy separate from money and the market-place, commercial philosophy looks here to stay. If this is so, then to try and stop this practical turn in philosophy would be to spit in the wind.

To pursue philosophy as 'a way of life' in the classical sense meant by Hadot is perhaps too unrealistic to expect in a complex modern world which is a far cry from ancient Athens with its charmed circle of some 100 or so elite philosophers. The institutionalisation of philosophy in modernity has ensured that there are many more philosophers than that number seeking employment today in the West. The home of philosophy for so many years was that educational institution of the state, the university college, which has turned out hundreds of philosophy graduates over the years, only a small proportion of whom can expect to secure an academic appointment. It is important to be realistic about the conditions of modern life, therefore.

What is more, if the 1999 UK Reith Lecturer is correct in his predictions about trends to globalisation in late modernity, then business prospects for the philosophical counselling of individuals should be bright (cf. Giddens 1999). The modernist sociologist Anthony Giddens argued in these lectures that with the decline of faith and tradition in late modernity and the growth of risk and choice of many types, individuals have become increasingly alone and insecure. There is 'no expert of experts' to whom they can turn. They have two avenues open to them: they can try to escape into some form of addiction (which he also calls 'frozen autonomy') or they can seek emancipation as self confident 'skilled and knowledgeable' autonomous agents. His prescription for those who choose the latter course is a fashionable one: to follow a course of counselling or psychotherapy. (Although PC as an alternative to psychological forms of counselling presumably never occurred to Giddens).

Qualified psychologists, and therapists and counsellors unqualified in psychology who have followed a different professional path, have propogated types of counselling and psychotherapy of many varied hues since Freud, usually on a one-to-one level and sometimes in group sessions. In the West, counselling has become a fashionable pursuit among the middle classes; almost an obsession for some we could say. We live in a culture of therapy and therapising. To the sceptic and the cynic, commercialised PC could be seen as yet another jump onto a fashionable commercial bandwagon; as yet another form of modern exploitation.

On the other hand, the technique of 'cognitive behaviour therapy' which is commonly practised in the National Health Service (NHS) by UK clinical psychologists, and which examines a client's beliefs and causal attributions before seeking to change 'unhealthy' thoughts and attitudes, looks rather like doing philosophy. It is not dissimilar to ancient philosophy, to the Stoics' injunction, for example, that the first step in philosophy was to accept the distinction between 'things which are in our power' (to change) and those which are not. There are echoes here of 'Alcoholics Anonymous'. If philosophers are becoming more like psychologists, it has to be said that psychology has borrowed from philosophy. There is no space in this article to pursue this interesting question of content overlap between the two disciplines of psychology and philosophy — merely to note that it exists.

In modernity psychology became institutionalised and bureaucratised as did sociology, and philosophy, and as did science. Psychologists became servants of the state. As agents of the state psychologists in Britain became university teachers, NHS clinicians, or educational psychologists in state schools, and some became servants of industry and commerce, usually as aides to management. As public servants they were in danger of losing their autonomy and becoming obsessed with careers and reputations. As servants of industry they were also at risk of becoming obsessed with money.

One social commentator, the American George Ritzer, views late modernity as the 'McDonaldisation' of society (Ritzer 1992).[5] In an open letter just prior to the Leusden conference a German Socratic, Ute Siebert, issued a challenge to the Dutch Socratic Jos Kessels in which she invited him to defend his use of modern SD in the market-place against the charge of McDonaldisation. In response Jos Kessels arranged a public debate on this theme at the Leusden event which included his challenger on the one side, with Jos Kessels himself on the other accompanied by an organisational psychologist colleague of his, and a branch manager of the Dutch Cooperative Bank who is one of Jos' clients. We felt that since the debate is important and met with only limited success at Leusden that it merited continuation in a more thorough manner in the future. The Loccum event provided that forum two years later, and this volume of the Schriftenreihe is dedicated to that conference.

In Ritzer's view, sociology had become factory-like and routinized. Securing a comfortable lifestyle and professional status, rather than seeking to change the world for the better, is the over-riding goal of the social sciences professional in the modern world, according to this perspective. Of course, the true picture is more complicated than the above might suggest. Many applied organisational psychologists, for example, are people of competence and goodwill. Sometimes they have found themselves out of their depth, out of naivety about organisational politics, or because of the sheer complexity of the situations in which they found themselves. This has often led to them feeling abused as tools of management, tools of public sector management as well as private sector. Many others, on the other hand, are completely at ease in that role. Yet others have been able to contribute to individual well-being and to more humane as well as more efficient conditions of work. We perhaps could say the same of the Dutch Socratics who have turned management consultants.

---

5   In a paper written by one of the present authors (PS) „Psychology and work; the growth of a discipline" (in: Canter, S.; Canter, D. (eds.) 1982) the point was to warn novices to the profession of the traps for the unwary into which the naïve could fall. The author herself had fallen into some of these traps during many years of application in the field. Applied psychologists had been trained and socialised in earlier days to believe that they were objective scientists in a value-free discipline. But we ignore the many different interests of those involved in the field at our peril.

Becoming Professional

In his analysis of the sociology of professions which still has relevance for professional practice today, Johnson pointed to what he saw as a neglected variable — the power relations between the professions and society. He drew attention to the two-faced Janus-like quality of professionalisation (Johnson 1972).[6] Is professionalisation intended to protect the public from the unscrupulous and the charlatan, or to protect the status, market territory and privileges of the professional? Two of Johnson's distinguished predecessors in sociology, Emile Durkheim and Talcott Parsons, had earlier taken a more benign view of the professions as moral communities. With the decline of traditional morality in modernity Durkheim envisaged professional ethics as the foundation of a new moral order. This faith in the professionals' ethic of service for the common good was shared by Parsons (Parsons 1954, pp. 34-49).[7]

2001 is the centenary of the British Psychological Society (BPS) which was founded in 1901, and was incorporated by Royal Charter in 1965. The BPS has become increasingly professionalised over the years, so much so that qualified practioners now may enjoy chartered status. The Society is also soon likely to obtain statutory registration for qualified members. Talks with government are well advanced in relation to the British government's new Health Bill, which contains a clause enabling the introduction of statutory regulation of relevant professions. Psychology is seen as one of the professional groups concerned with the health of individuals. That would bring the status of British psychologists more in line with German psychologists, with those in Holland where 'psychologist' is a protected title, and with professional psychologists in some other countries.

Over the 100 years of its history the discipline has splintered into sub-disciplines, creating a tension between the need for central unity and the push to specialise. There is an older tension between academic psychologists (the teachers and researchers) and the practitioners. In fact,

---

6   See also Marinoff op. cit.

7   The most famous source of Durkheim's hopes for professional ethics as a moral guide to society at large is of course his dissertation (Durckheim 1893). Readers may also wish to refer to his posthumous Lecons de sociologie. (Durckheim 1950).

it was pressure on the Society from the clinicals working alongside psychiatrists in the National Health Service which drove the professionalisation of the discipline. There was also external pressure from the prospect of litigation, and public and state interest stirred up by occasional legal and disciplinary cases of unethical practice and client abuse.[8]

The case for statutory legislation to cover qualified psychologists specialising in clinical therapy and other practitioners offering counselling, as a means of protecting the public interest, is strengthened by the 'rise and rise' of the broad counselling movement. Much counselling is now done in an unregulated manner, by the unqualified or under-qualified. The philosophical counsellor may sometimes be seen (perhaps unfairly) as falling into this latter category; as potentially capable of abuse of innocent clients because of inadequate training. It may not then constitute sufficient defence to argue that PC does not entail psychological issues or the need to protect the defenceless client from abuse by the unqualified philosophy practitioner.

SD and PC practitioners may well come across emotional problems in their practice. How far are they prepared for this? More may be expected from them than to engage purely in logic and dialectic. Many individual 'intrapsychic' problems may arise among SD participants inadvertently, even with a very experienced facilitator, as may destructive group dynamics. Birnbacher (op. cit.) seems to gloss over these issues and to base his paper on work with students in sheltered settings who have already learnt to work together. But it doesn't appear realistic to split 'the client' up as someone with a separate psychological versus a

---

8   In one case a Fellow of the British Psychological Society withdrew from the clinical register on being found guilty of gross professional misconduct. That he was not also dismissed from membership stirred up a hornet's nest among the ranks who expressed deep concern about what could be construed as ineffectual professional self-regulation at a time when it is known that the British government intends to modernise existing therapy regulatory arrangements, with particular reference (but not only) to the NHS. Given his voluntary undertaking to never again practise, the Disciplinary Committee of the Society claimed it had acted on the assumption that it would lose all power to exert some control over the Fellow's behaviour if he were to be expelled outright.

For a fuller discussion of the case see Lunt 1999, p. 59 (and the following page of the journal for members' correspondence on the case). See also Jopling 1997.

philosophical side. After all, individual people are all of a piece. Cognitions and emotions, thoughts and feelings, are intertwined. It is the academic disciplines and the professions that are fragmented. There is also the tricky issue of the notion of the subconscious mind, but there is no space in this paper to do justice to that complex topic.

Professionally, the applied psychologist is expected to know when she is out of her depth (to know herself) and to know when and how to refer the client on — to a physician or psychiatrist, for example. Furthermore, many organic medical conditions present as psychological disturbances. For example, as many as 10% of individuals with mild to moderate depression who present to psychiatrists or psychologists and psychotherapists have an underactive thyroid, which is a potentially dangerous physical condition. Thyroid medication is more likely to benefit them than is existential discourse about the meaning of life and death or engaging solely in a Socratic Dialogue process of regressive abstraction.

At present it is a matter of *caveat emptor,* although this may change, in the UK and throughout the European Union, if psychologists win the day in achieving statutory protection. What then will practitioners of commercialised SD and PC do? Will they also travel down this long, expensive and difficult professional road? The future for them is as yet too uncertain for an answer to this question. The incoherence of PC and the ambiguous definitions of its practice domain (its claim to particular and unique expertise) implies that the potential for practical philosophy to become professionalised is not wholly out of the question. One recent edition of 'Practical Philosophy' (Vol. 3, 2, July 2000) contains contributions discussing this very topic of problematic definition in PC. The dangers to the public presented by unqualified practitioners of PC may not however, on the face of it, apply to practitioners of commercially applied SD, but here again we are faced with ambiguity.

The pressures on European, and American, psychologists in qualifying and in continuing professional development are already substantial and standards are high. Their entry to the profession is regulated, as is their training and examination. Respectable accredited and certified counsellors who are not qualified as psychologists, with whom some practising philosophers prefer to identify, are also expected in the UK to undertake intensive prolonged therapy themselves and to practise under continual supervision. In truth, psychologists have far less status and power than medical practitioners and just as much of the bureaucratic paraphernalia.

It is not suggested that practising philosophers will, of necessity, become professionalised, or indeed that they should. This fate may eventually befall them, however — unless they can show that they are not in the business of influencing people's health. Suffice to mention that practical philosophers, PC practitioners in particular, may be obliged to join doctors and applied psychologists in cleaning up their acts.

The Dutch Socratics have gone on to develop their own training programmes for Socratic Dialogue facilitators and for philosophical counselling. In Britain a 'Society of Consultant Philosophers' (SCP) was founded in 1995 as a British wing of the Dutch Association for Philosophical Practice (VFP) by a Dutch Socratic who is resident in Britain, which became independent in 1998 and offered training and consultancy in PC and in versions of the Nelson-Heckmann SD. A national register of practitioners who had fulfilled the SCP's own eligibility and training requirements and who subscribed to the Society's own ethical code of practice was set up. A further initiative was the publication of its own journal: 'Practical Philosophy'.

The Ethical Path

'First do no harm.' (The Hippocratic Oath of medical ethics)

In medicine physicians have a paramount duty of care for their patients. 'Above all do no harm' is the ethical principle of 'non maleficence' in medicine. The mental and emotional health of vulnerable individuals seeking counselling help from unqualified practitioners is of growing concern in the UK. The central issue is the abuse of clients in its various forms, especially sexual abuse in one-to-one 'dual relationships'.

If philosophers wish to make a living from philosophy they may also want to learn something valuable from other relevant disciplines, from practitioners in psychology and medicine, for example, who have been in the game longer, about dealing with the pitfalls and perils of practising in the outside world. Indeed, that most revered of practising philosophers, Socrates himself, suggested that ignorance alone can be the cause of vicious action. In fact, there are also many traps for the practitioner in the field who is not in anyone's pay. Neither paid practitioners nor voluntary practitioners are exempt. Practise in the market-place may present especial problems for the former, however, if they are paid by and on behalf of organisations; a risk that may apply less to those only paid by individual fee-paying clients. The former, we might suppose, exchange their autonomy to a not inconsiderable degree for services which have been bought by their paymasters in the organisation. (The questionable degree of autonomy enjoyed by academic teachers of philosophy is a separate, though not irrelevant, issue).

The level of professional protection enjoyed by applied psychologists and their clients has been hard won over many years, after much soul-searching and voluntary effort on the part of some individual psychologists and their professional committees. Ethics is now accepted as a central issue for professional psychology. The BPS has a 'Professional Affairs Board', an 'Ethics Committee', 'Code of Ethical Conduct' and an 'Investigating Committee & Disciplinary Board'.

The matter does not stop at the door of the counsellor's room. Educational and work (organisational/occupational) psychologists are increasingly concerned with their own professional ethics. If actions have been brought against clinical and counselling therapists for individual client abuse, accusations of 'management lackey' have been aimed at specialists in work psychology, often with some justification because they have tended to take the management's rather than the workers' side — usually because management, as fee payer, was the piper who called the tune.

Some of us may be coy about taking up an overt ethical stance. We may fear ridicule or scorn in a wider culture which espouses macho enterprise and risk-taking on the one hand or is quick to 'call the kettle black' on the other. None of us is perfect and it would be quite rare and incredible if we were not sometimes unethical in our lives. Besides, 'to err is human'. Many ordinary people will struggle with this 'goody two shoes' sensibility and 'goodness is smugness' image, especially when confronted with those common grey areas of moral ambiguity. After all, ambiguous grey areas are the rule rather than the exception in organisational and professional life.

Many of us enjoy the protection of a professional body. A professional body undergoes a maturing process over many years of practise and the professional institution is a potential source of ethical socialisation and training, as well as protection for its members. Ethical codes of professional practice are only the start. Unless an unethical practice becomes overt and a matter for internal professional discipline or, worse, for public litigation, everyday ethical practise is a matter of covert personal decision and choice, of individual conscience.

We may be well acquainted with ethical theory, but ethics in practice is a different matter altogether, and much ethical consciousness and competence is learnt on the job, conditions permitting. Whether their business commitments these days will allow practical philosophers, and applied psychologists, to give the necessary reflection to their practice, in a climate and context in which 'time is money', whether it will rob them of that freedom for critique, of that reflective capacity, is not for us to judge.

As we reflect on these things, perhaps we need always to bear in mind that a person or a method that has the capacity to do great good has also, and by the same token, the capacity to do great harm. Plato had much earlier warned us about the perils of possessing skills and knowledge. The subsequent events over the many centuries since have confirmed the inherent ambiguity of all things, often horrifyingly so. Practical and applied philosophy, like applied psychology, even if ethical, is not excluded from this general condition. 'The road to hell is paved with good intentions', as we were reminded by the good Dr Johnson.

Naivety about the potential for evil, even at the heart of philosophy and ethics, can be very dangerous indeed. But this does not mean that we should renounce their potential for good. Far from it. Only vigilance, however, constant and exquisite vigilance, and critique about our ways and means can be of help here; if they can't quite save us, they may at least keep us from harm.

Practitioners of all stripes have also felt the need for outside independent protection from professional conflicts generated by the organisations that employ them. Clinical and counselling psychologists working alongside practitioners from other disciplines within the UK's NHS, and especially alongside psychiatrists, have felt the need for the protection afforded by their own external professional body. The manifest purpose of some kind of charter-cum-code is ethical, to protect society against abusive practitioners, but there is room for abuse in both directions. The charter also affords some protection to those ethical practitioners from employers who might abuse them, as well as from the unqualified who might be tempted to invade their area of professional expertise. Neither philosophers, nor psychologists, nor society are benign or malintended as such.

Getting involved in messy real world practice guarantees that frequent encounters with ethical issues are inevitable for practitioners. Practitioner awareness, willingness and competence to deal with such issues cannot be taken for granted, on the other hand. Many ethical issues will be latent rather than overt. Practical philosophers will be personally challenged on the job, and sometimes in public, to show where they stand on ethics. Indeed, it would seem anomalous if they failed to make their position clear, given the history of their discipline, and the fact that ethics is a main branch of philosophy.

Thinking and philosophy are for a purpose, but for what and whose purpose merits consideration. Whatever the primary pursuit of an organisation, whether profit-making business or public sector charity, the organisation's purpose is always a moral and ethical one. And if the organisation is able to be other things at the same time as being moral, to be efficient and so on, then so much the better. This has been shown time and time again to be the case, even for economic enterprise, by sociologists of rank, from Max Weber (Weber 1920) on to Robert Wuthnow (Wuthnow 1996).

Many of us in these days of late capitalism are suffering a postmodern anomie, a kind of debilitating malaise. Many others are burning themselves out in dual or multiple mandate jobs in the service of systems which perpetuate a destructive status quo in Giddens' 'runaway world'. Sometimes it feels as if we are in danger of society existing for the purpose of business, rather than business (and other organisations) existing to serve society and the 'good life' of its citizens. The modern state seems to have become more a burden on its citizens than a benefit. Sure, philosophers, like psychologists need to eat, to 'keep body and soul together'. Will they though, philosophers and psychologists, remain part of the problem or can they, will they, contribute to its solution?

Will practical philosophers take their place alongside applied psychologists to try and make our world a better place, and be mutuallysupportive in this cause as friends and colleagues?

Unlike the modern profession of psychology, individual practitioner psychologists, like many other practitioners, may not automatically include ethics in their practice. Psychologists could do with some help from philosophy, and probably the reverse is true. Philosophers, unlike psychologists for example, are not usually trained in empirical research, and this skill may be an added value for their profession. Mutual support between complementary, not competing, disciplines we surmise could reduce the stress of the practising members in each, and can only be to the ultimate good of those meant to benefit from their services.

There is room for both disciplines. Indeed some of us may want to say that there is a growing need for individuals who have a strong sense of the ethical who are also willing to get their hands dirty in complex reality. Their competence and courage are needed to help people to become more like Giddens' 'skilled and knowledgeable agents' in the contemporary 'runaway' global world.

Hadot (op. cit.) wrote: 'In ancient philosophy (…) an essential place is accorded to the duty always to act in the service of the human community, that is, to act in accordance with justice.' Some psychologists, like some doctors and managers, had lost sight of ethics; had neglected the highest good in their other pursuits. The eighteenth century German philosopher Immanuel Kant believed that what we have lost and abandoned we have the capacity to restore, and Leonard Nelson not only shared this view, he devoted his life in trying to promote it in practise.

Where then does contemporary practical philosophy position itself in this debate? Traditionally the three main branches of philosophy are: what exists (ontology); what we know (epistemology); and what is good/right (ethics). Given this tradition is it not reasonable to expect an ethical consciousness and ethical practice from all applied philosophers? And is it not indeed reasonable to expect those who apply philosophy using techniques such as the Socratic Dialogue, which are the heritage of forebears for whom philosophy was 'a way of life', to be especially sensitive to their potential for abuse; to be especially concerned about their own responsibility for the promotion of the highest good?

A further turn-back to something rather closer to the idea of philosophy as a way of life but updated to take account of modern conditions — may be essential to help reverse some of the destructive trends of late modernity. We think it doesn't have to be a matter of philosophy applied for *either* private profit *or* public good, so long as practitioners are eternally vigilant and try to avoid doing harm to others.

Harm will sometimes be done unwittingly, because of the messiness of the world, and because of our all too human limitations.

It is also possible that those practitioners taking fees for their services may be more at risk of doing harm than might the unpaid volunteer, but this is not inevitable. We can cultivate the virtues of vigilance and humility, however, and treat with all seriousness the need to become ethical, skilled and knowledgeable agents ourselves, as applied philosophers or psychologists. Indeed, the need has never been more pressing.

References

Baggini, Julian (1999): Life on the Fringe. In: The Philosophers' Magazine, 8, pp. 11-12.

Birnbacher, Dieter (1999): The Socratic method in teaching medical ethics: potentials and limitations. In: Medicine, Health Care and Philosophy, *2*, pp. 219-224.

Durckheim, Max (1893): De la division du travail social. Paris: Alcan.

Durckheim, Max (1950): Lecons de sociologie. Paris: Presses Universitaires de France.

Giddens, Anthony (1999): Runaway World: how globalisation is shaping our lives. [The Runaway World. BBC Reith Lectures.] London: Profile Books.

Goord, Margaret (1998): Philosophical Practice: the case against. In: The New York Times 8. 3.

Hadot, Pierre (1995): Philosophy as a Way of Life: spiritual exercises from Socrates to Foucault. Translated by Michael Chase. Oxford: Blackwell.

Van Hooft, Stan (2000): Report from Loccum. In: Practical Philosophy, 3 (3), pp. 75-77.

Johnson, Terence J. (1972): Professions and Power. London: Macmillan.

Jopling, D. (1997): First do no harm. Over-philosophising and pseudo-philosophising in philosophical counselling. In: Inquiry, 17 (2).

Kessels, Jos (1997): Socrates op de markt. Filosofie in bedrijf. Amsterdam/Mechelen: Boom.

Leal, Fernando; Shipley, Patricia (2002): From value conflicts to multiple mandates: organising ethical knowledge and its paradoxes. Chapter 7. In: S. R. Clegg (ed.) Management and Organiszation Paradoxes . Amsterdam/Philadelphia: John Benjamins, pp.136-161.

LeBon, Tim (2000): The Clinic. The Philosophers' Magazine, 10, p. 27.

Lunt, Ingrid (1999): Disciplining psychologists. The President's Column. In: The Psychologist, 12, 2, p. 59.

Mason, Marilyn (2000), Opinion. In: The Philosophers' Magazine 9, p.8.

Parsons, Talcott (1954): The Professions and Social Structure. In: Essays in Sociological Theory. Glencoe, Ill., pp. 34-49.

Ritzer, George (1992): The McDonaldization of Society. Newbury Park, CA: Sage.

Scruton, Roger (1997): The Return of the Sophist. In: The Times, London, 11 August.

Shipley, Patricia (1982): Psychology and work; the growth of a discipline. In: S. Canter; D. Canter (eds.): Psychology in Practice: Perspectives on Professional Practice. Chichester: John Wiley, pp. 165-176.

Stangroom, Jeremy (1998): What do philosophical practitioners do? In: Philosophers' Magazine 3, p. 36.

Weber, Max (1920): Essays on the Sociology of Religion. Tübingen: Mohr.

Wuthnow, Robert (1996): Poor Richard's Principle: Recovering the American Dream through the Moral Dimension of Work, Business, and Money. New Yersey: Princeton: University Press.

(NB: This contribution was based on a paper by the authors 'Is practical philosophy for private profit or public good?: a critical view of the practical turn in contemporary philosophy' which was published in the Journal Philosophy in the Contemporary World, 9, 1, spring-summer 2001, pp.1-9.)

Pat Shipley

Getting Excited about Emotions[1]

The contemporary Socratic Dialogue, the Nelson-Heckmann dialogue
which originated in Germany, is philosophical enquiry in a group setting.
Each separate dialogue is an attempt at forming a community of enquiry,
or thinking as a group, which is an important part of the whole process.
Each individual participant brings with her to the group her own
background and history, her particular fears, motives and desires.
Participants bring feelings of empathy, sympathy, or even antipathy. To
use the jargon they bring their own 'emotional baggage'. There is much
more going on in the process than purely addressing a philosophical
question in a cool, detached and rational manner. There is feeling as well
as thinking, passion as well as reason. But these feelings can be pushed
aside, become peripheral or repressed. This short paper is stimulated by
two questions. How open is/can a Socratic Dialogue be? How can it be
deepened and developed psychologically? The aim is to bring
psychological influences in the dialogue into greater awareness. It is
proposed that a greater understanding of these psychological, specifically
emotional, issues would enrich the process of dialogue.

Reason the Charioteer

Socrates is often accused of intellectualising, but Plato, the master
dramatist, conveys feeling and passion in his Dialogues as well as
intellectual and rational features. Indeed, Socrates intended the
experience of dialogue to transform the whole person; one's whole way
of life. Participation in the dialogue was not a game to be treated lightly

1   The collaboration of Loes de Jong, Socratic facilitator from Holland, is
     acknowledged in the preparation for this paper.

or which could be forgotten about on leaving. The injunction was to "Know thyself", and "The unexamined life is not worth living". Socrates' own choice of metaphors for his own role in the dialogues (that of the midwife and the gadfly) vividly portray this potentially painful process.

This painful experience was particularly likely to occur in the first phase of the classical dialogue, the phase of '*elenchus*'. This was the period of embarrassment and self-doubt as Socrates' pupils were trapped in their contradictions, and their conceits, prejudices, and inconsistencies remorselessly exposed in the public gaze under his skilful questioning. There was a deep emotional risk to the person participating in the dialogue. Socrates wanted to analyse whole lives, not merely words. How, therefore, could the dialogues be free of passion, when one's cherished values and even one's whole belief system could be under attack, or, conversely, when the 'truth' was finally and joyfully revealed after the many dialectical twists and turns in the dialogue and after much delving?

Plato has his own colourful metaphor for the disciplined and controlled management of the emotions during dialogue (in fact, during one's whole life). It is the image of Reason as a charioteer riding across the heavens in a cavalcade of the gods with the reins of the good and docile white horse of courage or spirit in one hand and in the other the reins of the wild and evil black horse of passion. Plato was of course no stranger to the Greek Tragedies. His metaphor of the tripartite soul was borrowed over 2000 years later by Freud, the father of psychoanalysis. Plato cultivated an other-worldly metaphysical vision which was at odds with the prevailing values of heroic passion, utter ruthlessness, unbridled ambition, banal greed and lust, and petty pride in the Athens of his day.

The Nelsonians, the ethical socialist group formed in the first half of last century in Germany, seemed to be oblivious of the power of emotions. Their leader, the German Kantian philosopher, Leonard Nelson, was himself silent about the practical importance of emotions for philosophy. He may even have denied them to himself, except he is known to have been a very passionate man in his private life.[2] His disciple, Gustav Heckmann, who after Nelson's death went on to develop the Socratic method originated by Nelson, acknowledged their

2   This refers to what he says about Socrates and the method. Nelson's full account of this topic elsewhere is complicated and ambivalent, his 'sittliches Interesse' being intellectual rather than practical (Fernando Leal, personal communication).

existence and relevance for the Nelsonian dialogue but confined himself to writing only a few bland statements about emotions. He split them off from the main dialogue process by banishing them to his invention, the 'metadialogue', in which any "discomfort should be articulated" within Socratic groups which may involve "inchoate feelings of stress or confusion caused by the intensity of our enquiry". (Heckmann 1987, p. 34-37) This splitting manoeuvre is an interesting expression of a long-lived tendency we have for dualistic thinking; the reason-emotion dualism, for example, having permeated western tradition since the early Greeks.

In his 'preconditions' for participation in Socratic Dialogue Heckmann did not explicitly identify emotional maturity as a criterion for participation. Yet there must have been such a presumption. For Heckmann *individual* psychic problems are excluded' from the dialogue because, he argued, they could only be dealt with by psychoanalysis, not through philosophising. Nelson, who was a contemporary of Freud, had ignored Freud, and seemed indifferent to psychology as such, a subject which had just begun to take off on the Continent. Experimental psychology is traditionally deemed to have begun in Wundt's laboratory in Leipzig at the turn of the century. Perhaps the assumption was that philosophy took care of reason and psychology was about the emotions.

A contemporary Socratic, Fernando Leal, has reminded us recently of the centrality of the emotions during the classical Socratic Dialogue:

> "(…) people got excited, they got angry, they got elated. As you know, Socrates was killed by the government. But he was not killed just because he was an egghead who asked uncomfortable questions. Intellectualistic eggheads don't generally get themselves executed. Socrates awoke very powerful emotions; and our own Socratic Dialogue should do so too. If it doesn't, then we can be sure there is something wrong in the way we are doing it….(A)s each step in our analysis is carried out, we are not only thinking but *feeling* our way to the principle." (Leal 1998, p. 38)

Other statements about feelings encountered in the Nelson-Heckmann form of dialogue came to light that were made by three other contemporary dialogue facilitators:

"During a Socratic dialogue psychological problems or processes related to group dynamics may have a negative influence on the progress of the dialogue."

"Any feeling of discomfort which disturbs the dialogue proper should be expressed."

"….dissatisfaction with the course of events is often projected upon the facilitator. He shouldn't be placed in a position in which he needs to defend himself (…)."

Dieter Birnbacher, a member of the German Academy (PPA) and a Socratic facilitator, has recently published a valuable article on the Nelsonian-Heckmann Socratic Dialogue (see Birnbacher 1999). His few statements in the paper about the emotional side of the dialogue, however, appear a little thin and anodyne. They reflect the ideal situation — or perhaps the safe confines of the university student group where students and teacher have become comfortable with each other. To quote him:

"On the affective side, participation in a Socratic group is a particularly satisfactory experience of an equilibrium of rationality and matter-of-factness on the one hand and of warmth, acceptance and openness on the other hand. On the cognitive side, it is an exercise in rational problem solution in a framework of strict discipline and restraint. On the affective side, it allows, within the supportive framework of the group, to gain an understanding of some of one's own inner conflicts, to control one's own self-perception by the feedback given by others and to identify empathically with the thinking and feeling of others." (Birnbacher 1999, p. 223)

Note the dualistic thinking in the distinction made above by Birnbacher in his description between the 'cognitive' and the 'affective' sides of the process. I am indebted at this point to the observation made my colleague Fernando Leal (in personal communication) that Jakob Friedrich Fries — through whose philosophy Nelson came to Kant — conceived of the distinction between conscious and unconscious thought processes, which Fries called 'higher' and 'lower' thought processes. Fernando Leal went on to observe that Fries' emphasis, as has always been the case with the Critical Philosophy, was on the 'higher' cognitive side, rather than the affective 'lower' side. Although Fries' dualism is strongly reminiscent of Freud's primary and secondary thought processes the connection between the Critical Philosophy and psychology at all is much stronger with that branch of psychology referred to by psychologists as 'cognitive' than it has been with other kinds of psychology.

The Modern World and its Commercial Exploitation of Emotions

"Now girls, I want you to go out there and really *smile*. Your smile is your biggest asset. I want you to go out there and use it. Smile. *Really* smile. Really *lay it on*." (Hochschild 1983)

We have posed a question about the taken-for-granted openness of the contemporary Socratic Dialogue. In fact, we do not usually know the emotional status of individual participants at the start of or during the course of the dialogue. It is not often transparent. Indeed, we do not know much about what goes on in the process philosophically, as well as psychologically. Is there an 'elenchus', for example, how far is consensus reached, what are the emotional blocks to good dialogue, does the personal style — and feelings — of the facilitator exert an important influence? It may seem that facilitators in the Nelson-Heckmann tradition expect the group participant to arrive at the dialogue as an emotional tabula rasa, or at least emotionally mature.

The assumption is that participants turn up to the dialogue as rational beings with their emotions under control, and no doubt many do. Many individuals undoubtedly experience good feelings about Socratic Dialogues, to which they return and re-experience from year to year, which is, many would surely believe, an adequate testimony to their value. Anecdotes suggest, on the other hand, that the dialogue may generate difficult emotional experiences for some individuals. This may arise as a result of the psychological dynamics in operation in their particular group, destructive group dynamics, or for some other reason. The facilitator may have difficulty dealing with the situation. The group's effort to accomplish the philosophical task may be thwarted because of emotional problems, (leaving problems of a *cognitive* psychological kind aside).

It may help to think in terms of the familiar three levels of analysis: the individual, the group, and the organisation. An *individual* may have personal problems which disrupt any group structure; at the *group* level the particular dynamics of the group may in itself be a source of problems; at the higher level each group is usually a part of a wider '*organisation*' and culture. It may be wise to assume that the boundaries between the group and organisation are quite permeable even if group participants try to keep their own group proceedings confidential. It is rather like a nest of Chinese boxes or Russian dolls. Another model is the open systems model. This model suggests that the organisational boundaries of the group are open to the wider society and culture so that the prevailing values and beliefs of the latter would be brought into the Socratic 'organisation' and to its constituent groups. The individual Socratic group is a small quasi-informal group — a temporary organisation — and participants come from common and from different cultures. The Nelson-Heckmann dialogue is already pre-structured along traditional lines, with its own rules, and based on pre-given traditional 'values', such as the values and doctrine of the founder, and these are an important part of the overall picture.

As for the wider scene many critics these days (and ordinary people) are concerned about the major social and economic problems of 'late modernity'. They talk of over-dependence on technology, a crisis of employment in terms of the quality and quantity of jobs, the tensions between fragmentation and globalization, and the seemingly Americanisation of an amoral world. For the question of global Americanisation see the ideas of George Ritzer (1998). Over-rationalisation may have produced a de-humanised world. The British sociologist, Anthony Giddens, calls this big picture 'The Runaway World', although he takes a weakly optimistic view of its future (Giddens 1999).

This wider scenario has generated many heated and other negative emotions. It may have relevance for the modern Socratic movement when the Nelson-Heckmann dialogue is being transposed from its traditional settings into business organisations. If this is important to modern Socratics do they feel they are part of the problem or a tiny and modest part of its solution?[3] For Nelson, these questions would surely

---

3   See open letter to Jos Kessels from Ute Siebert of the GSP, 1998.

have been relevant. He was concerned to put ethics into practice and saw his invention, the Socratic Dialogue, as an ethical and political tool for attaining this goal.

Nelson was part of the growing rationalisation of the age; he was of his time and place. Reason and rationality had been valorised in the west for centuries, and, some would want to say, to the detriment of emotional life. 'Instrumental rationality' reached its apotheosis in its excessive deployment in modern work systems with the over-specialisation and over-simplification of work in 'junk jobs'. It is now said that we have spent more effort on suppressing, or exploiting feelings than on developing them. The commercial world in the west was not slow to catch up with this idea and is now busy with the emotional manipulation of work forces, particularly those in the growing sector of close-customer-contact service jobs. Labour is being taught to use rigid scripts with consumers; tightly-controlled prescriptions or verbal routines which reflect inauthentic 'emotion' rather than the real thing.

In her study of female airline flight attendants, the American social scientist, Arlie Hochschild pioneered research into what she referred to as 'emotional labor'. A new industry has developed in the training of emotional management and the use by employers of emotional control techniques with the labour force. Once pre-occupied with intelligence tests of IQ the interest of management has broadened to include the emotional quotient (EQ). In his best seller Daniel Goleman regards EQ as a set of skills to be trained which consists of a number of abilities: self-perception, self-control, empathy and social skills (Goleman 1997).

One recent claim is that EQ "accounts for 87.5% of what sets outstanding performers apart from the average." (Comment in: The Psychologist 1999, 12, 10 p. 522) As critical philosophers we could ask ourselves how far this activity is open to abuse. Emotional labour might fool the consumer but it can create job stress. Emotional management, like rational thinking, is to a purpose. For whose purpose and in whose interest? Emotional intelligence like rational intelligence, is open to abuse. Both are two-edged swords.

Freeing the Emotions

But after all individual people are 'all of a piece'. It is the disciplines and the dualisms which fragment us. For the little known Scottish philosopher, John Macmurray (1891-1976) emotional maturity was an important part of a comprehensive rationality and a fully-rounded humanity (Macmurray 1935). There comes a time, he suggested, when thought cannot be free until feeling is free. But we distrust our emotions. We have set the intellect free and kept the emotions in chains, believing in freedom of thought but not of feeling. Instead Macmurray believed we should rely more on the acknowledgement and expression of honest authentic feelings and understand their role in practical reason and ethical conduct. He also believed that to be emotionally undisciplined is not to be free. As a Kantian he felt strongly that we need to submit to feelings which have been disciplined not by external authority but by and for ourselves, in the personal service of practical reason. Emotions may be put to good effect — perhaps in the service of practical ethics in organisations, in the development of '*arete*' (moral excellence) in the individual, and in other ways.

Several years after Macmurray died, the American sociologist, George Ritzer, issued a dire warning, that there is a subtle form of self-policing in the modern world. Even consumers — not just labourers — have so internalised 'McDonaldized' values that we discipline and self-regulate ourselves unthinkingly in the service of capitalism at the expense of our true selves. For a long time the two domains had been de-coupled; the emotional/interpersonal and the rational/technical. The ancient Greeks led us to believe that the one domain is feminine and the other is masculine, the one is inferior and the other superior. Aristotle is notorious for this. This is a mistake. Neither province is the sole prerogative of one sex. The duality was misleadingly expressed as in hierarchical opposition. Emotion is not the opposite or inferior partner of rationality or reason.

It is in the real world of practice that the falsity of this deep duality becomes evident. Yes, it is true, we sometimes act blindly and on emotional impulse and this is sometimes the wrong move. Often, though, our emotions are the only basis on which to act — because there is insufficient time to do otherwise and barely time to reflect, or when the situation is too complex, and when we are faced with an irresolvable dilemma between two 'right' actions, and when we cannot find the words. The emotions can be important evaluative signals in their own right. They can signal danger when fear is aroused, or that things are not quite right when we feel unease and discomfort.

Leaving debates about evolution aside, emotional development, the development of the whole self may be viewed as a dynamic project. The self is continuously shaped and reshaped through interaction with others, through discourse and dialogue and other experiences, and through the self-reflection of inner dialogue and other 'spiritual exercises'. This paper finishes on a note of good sense and reasoning about emotions from one of today's foremost classical ethical scholars, the American Martha Nussbaum. Nussbaum rebuts the notion that the emotions are irrational, and like Leal reminds us that for the ancients the emotions are central to our lives (see Nussbaum 1994). For her the natural human response to the suffering and vulnerability of another sentient being must be compassion.

The British psychologist, Keith Oatley, ventures:

> "It is not wholly Quixotic, I think, to imagine teaching a course on the psychology of emotions in which Nussbaum's 'Therapy of Desire' is not just the starting point, but also the culmination to which the course would tend after a journey along highways and lanes (…). For Nussbaum not only provides a vision of why as academics, or as people, we might be interested in the emotions, but why emotions are of such importance. They are of importance because they are the very centre of human life." (Oatley 1997, p. 308)

Emotions are not just a nuisance to the Socratic Dialogue, to be denied or suppressed, or, at best to be relegated to the 'metadialogue', but are central to the process. Rules narrow down the process and the issues. Hidden assumptions about keeping emotions out of the picture can be oppressive to participants and impoverishing to the dialogue. It is high time to include the emotions in theorising about dialogue, along with the other usual intellectual concepts of 'reason', 'truth', 'consensus', 'regressive abstraction', 'judgement' and 'principles', and what not. It is time for Socratics to get excited about emotions.

References

Birnbacher, Dieter (1999): The Socratic Method in Teaching Medical Ethics: Potentials and Limitations. In: Medicine, Health Care and Philosophy 2, pp. 219-224.

Giddens, Anthony (1999): Runaway World. London: Profile Books.

Goleman, Daniel (1997): Working with Emotional Intelligence. New York: Broadway Books.

Heckmann, Gustav (1987): Socratic Dialogue. In: Thinking: The Journal of Philosophy for Children, 8 (1), pp. 34-37.

Hochschild, Arlie R. (1983): The Managed Heart: Commercialization of Human Feeling. Berkeley, CA: University of California Press.

Leal, Fernando (1998): The Future of the Critical Philosophy. In: P. Shipley (ed.): Occasional Working Papers in Ethics and the Critical Philosophy, 1. London: Society for the Furtherance of the Critical Philosophy.

Macmurray, John (1935): Reason and Emotion. London: Faber.

Nussbaum, Martha (1994): The Therapy of Desire: Theory and Practice in Hellenistic Ethics. Princeton , New Jersey: Princeton University Press.

Oatley, Keith (1997): Emotions and Human Flourishing. In: Cognition and Emotion, 11, (3), pp. 307-330.

Ritzer, George (1998): The McDonaldization Thesis: Explorations and Extensions. London: Sage.

Gisela Raupach-Strey

Basic Rules for Socratic Dialogue

These rules are constitutive for the paradigm of Socratic Dialogues in the tradition of Nelson-Heckmann.

1. As a rational human being, everyone willing and ready to respect the following rules is able to join in a Socratic Dialogue.

2. The aim of a Socratic Dialogue is to gain fundamental and general insights into a philosophical problem. The topic or question determines the problem.

3. The starting point of the Dialogue is an individual experience so that participants have a firm footing in things concrete.

4. More specifically, the aim of a Socratic Dialogue is recognition of truth with respect to the solution of the given problem. Any consensus reached among all participants must be based on their own insight and voluntary consent.

4.1 In a Socratic Dialogue there is no pressure to reach a decision or to engage in action. The inherent aim is to reach consensus about truth. For participants there is usually the additional aim of reasonable individual self-determination. According to context, this can be understood in a pedagogical or political sense, or in terms of the theory of education and learning.

5. Participants make an effort to clarify their own thoughts and use clear language to express them so that others can understand them.

6. Participants make an effort to listen attentively to understand the thoughts of others in the group, and to help others to clarify and formulate their thoughts in the best way which is possible. This is developing the Socratic 'skill of the midwife' (called 'maieutic').

7. All should express themselves as concisely as possible to contribute to the common search for truth on the given problem. Briefly: as much words as necessary, as few as possible.

8. Sincerity should underpin all statements or doubts expressed; at the point when contributions to the discussion are made the speaker should be ready to defend them with arguments.

9. Arguments used by individuals to defend particular propositions are of two kinds:

9.1 Abstract philosophical statements. These should be explained by way of concrete examples so that the listener is able to apply the test of understanding (according to Gustav Heckmann this is the 'Socratic Principle'). Insight into a general subject is possible only via examining and analysing a concrete experience subsumed to the general fact.

9.2 Conversely, the participants should not immerse themselves solely in the concrete experience, but should search for the underlying general principle and convictions by the process of 'regressive abstraction', and should examine these found generals.

10. Every Socratic Dialogue group is responsible in common for the process of recognition. Having moved from individual to more general statements, their validity has to be tested. The reasons for and against propositions have to be examined in common in as unprejudiced a way as possible. The Dialogue has to be exploited as an instrument for clarifying and deepening one's thoughts. All contradictions regarding the given topic and all objections raised by participants have to be examined until (if at all possible) they are resolved. Everyone has to decide honestly for herself/himself whether inner consent can be given.

11. The authority for the validity of arguments does not rest on
    - the view of a person or a group;
    - what has been read or heard;
    - a doctrine;
    but on
    - the self-confidence in reason;
    - the 'principle of reason', i.e. the peculiar 'forceless force' of the better argument. The consequence of these points is:

12. A readiness for revision: anyone who gains a new recognition, notices an old error or realises that an earlier contribution should be curtailed or modified, should be willing to communicate this to the others to advance the group's search for truth and to benefit the overall dialogue.

13. No force other than the force of reason is admissible in any part of the dialogue, neither direct, nor structural, and all participants should endeavour to shape the dialogue in conformity with the 'ideal situation of speech'.

14. Responsibility for the progress of the dialogue lies with the community of the group. Jointly everyone is responsible for fertile progress. Thus anyone is allowed to comment on the course and regulation of the dialogue; to ask for clarification in respect of any obscurity or confusion or of the actual point of the dialogue. [Sometimes such points are best raised in a Meta dialogue].

15. All participants (regardless of gender) have equal rights concerning the different types of contributions to the dialogue. The facilitator is temporarily responsible, with the agreement of the group, for ensuring that group members understand each other; that the inquiry is objective and that fruitful progress in the dialogue is achieved. As far as possible the facilitator renounces participating in matters of content during the dialogue. It is the task of all participants in the dialogue to treat each other with mutual respect and tolerance, so as to promote insights into the subject under examination.

Translated extract from the Essay by Gisela Raupach-Strey (1997): Grundregeln des Sokratischen Gesprächs. Vol. IV, Schriftenreihe der PPA, pp. 149-152.

Klaus Roß

What is an Argument?

The definition of a Socratic Dialogue (SD) given by Gustav Heckmann (1993, p. 13) is very broad. According to him every dialogue where arguments are brought forward and where people try to reach a consensus could be called a SD. In reality some restrictions are imposed on arguments for a proper SD (in the sense of a SD^{CP} described by Horst Gronke in his lecture). It may be some of the problems[1] dealt with in this article do only occur in a SD, as it *should* be practised the German way. A difficulty arises at this point because one would need a proper transcript (see 'Talking Data' edited by Jane Edwards) of the dialogue to analyse[2] the *real* arguments used by the participants. The formulations written down on the flipchart show only the tip of the iceberg in revealing what the participants regarded as worthwhile to be analysed. Minutes are not sufficient either because they lack a lot of information needed for the analysis of arguments brought forward during the dialogue.

It is necessary to distinguish between arguments and non-arguments. Utterances like requests, imperatives, threats[3] are sometimes used as 'supporting' statements to bring about the 'consensus' of others. These verbal means are not arguments because they are in no way related to the content of the sentence in question but aim instead only at the behaviour of other persons.

---

1 Due to language problems, some misunderstandings and a lack of time as well as some participants having to leave early we did not get very far in discussing the problems of argumentation in a Socratic Dialogue. Instead of simply reporting the meagre results of the group work I try to get across the main idea the workshop was aiming at and formulate some questions for the future work.

2 The points I want to make are only illustrated by examples I experienced in SDs.

3 'Threat' in this context does not mean threatening to harm an other person by physical force but using psychological force by pointing out that someone is holding up the whole group and preventing them from making progress.

To fulfil his task the facilitator has to recognize arguments either openly formulated as such or hidden in formulations that are not looking like an argument on first sight. The notion of an argument may be different for the participants and the facilitator. Depending on what one counts as an argument one might get the impression very few arguments were presented during a SD (cf. Raupach-Strey 1989, p. 41). On the other hand some participants may equate *every* statement with an argument as it happened during the workshop while a group was analysing an example of argumentation.

A general description (I hesitate to call it a definition) of argumentation is: *argumentation is the process that relates supporting sentences to a judgement.* This formulation tries to avoid the technical terms from logic[4] and could include different types of formulations. To understand an argument as 'a unit of thinking' (Coyne 1984, p. 2) leaves the way open for relating processes that are not included in definitions strictly orientated towards logical thinking. Often they are restricted to deduction and according to this concept formulations should follow the syllogistic pattern: major and minor premises lead to a conclusion. In reality people change the sequence of formulations (often with some unrelated sentences in between) and sometimes simply omit one of the premises altogether or even worse — they use formulations (e.g. proverbs or analogies) that do not fit into this neat pattern.

People don't label their expressions 'this is an argument'. The relation may be indicated by key words (like 'therefore' and 'since') but could also happen only in the head of the speaker and — if successful — in the head of the listeners. The difficulty of the relation between utterances in argumentation is similar to the problem of coherence. Neither is fixed in the sentences but in the communicators' (speakers' *and* listeners') minds (Givón 1995) and use the knowledge of the world. A speaker might see a very obvious connection between what he said in two sentences and for him one formulation is an argument in relation to the other while it is not for the listeners. Presuppositions play an important part in this process. The speaker takes for granted the listener will use the same

---

4   A definition in a recent book on argumentation defines 'argument' in the glossary as follows: "Folge von Sätzen, bestehend aus mindestens einer Prämisse und genau einer Konklusion. Die Prämissen (…) werden angeführt als Gründe, die Konklusion (…) zu akzeptieren." (Bayer 1999, p. 229)

presuppositions he does not spell out and will therefore be able to follow his thoughts. But even if the relation is stated openly the kind of connection is not always accepted. Only if listeners do recognise the relation between utterances are they able to treat formulations as an argument. The question whether an utterance counts as an argument should not be mixed up with the question whether it is a strong (convincing) argument. Recognising something as an argument does not necessarily mean the listener is convinced.

One does at least know where the difference lies and is able to bring forward doubts or counter-arguments and can try to reach a consensus. Only utterances fulfilling certain conditions are allowed to be used as arguments during a SD. In his welcome information, Dieter Krohn outlined the main rules to be followed in a SD. In the first rule for the facilitator a precondition for the consensus is formulated: 'Consensus is only achieved when contradictory points of view have been resolved *and all arguments and counter-arguments have been fully considered*; the facilitator has to ensure this happens.' (Krohn 2000, p. 4; emphasis added) I suppose this means all arguments formulated in the SD, not all arguments that could possibly be brought forward. Even if a statement will be considered as an argument by a lot of people, a participant taking part in a SD is not allowed to use it unless he believes in it himself. One major condition[5] for the speaker is his truthfulness. Therefore one is only allowed to formulate 'genuine doubt' (compare rule 2 in Krohn 2000, p. 4). It is not permitted to play the 'devil's advocate' in a SD (see Roß 1996).

The first of the basic rules for the participants requires him to refer only to his own experience: 'Each participant's contribution is based upon what s/he has experienced, *not upon what s/he has read or heard*.' (Krohn 2000, p. 4; emphasis mine) Already some years ago, Barbara Neißer (1989, p. 134) pointed out it may be problematic to limit a SD to one's own experience. It might be a good requirement for the choice of examples (to exclude examples based on imagining exotic situations) but the limit to one's own experience is difficult if applied to argumentation. How could I talk about something that does not stem from my experience of, for example, the power of institutions? If one were to

---

5 It is understood without questioning someone taking part in a SD lives up to this standard.

stick strictly to what one has experienced oneself and *all* 'second-hand' experiences were excluded argumentation would be very limited. A lot of events are only available to us via the media[6] or via dialogue with other people.

It is especially forbidden to refer to authorities[7] in a SD. Mistrust of authorities has led to a total ban of this type of arguments in the SD. I remember taking part in a SD with other facilitators which was on 'the limits of tolerance'. The example dealt with people on a train making too much noise. I used, as an argument to support my claim that their behaviour was unacceptable, a reference to the guidelines for travellers issued by the German Railway Company. Nobody complained about this use of a reference to an authority. Whether it is really possible to exclude authorities from all our statements (cf. Shaw 1997, p. 190) remains an open question.

A common way of describing, as well as arguing, is the use of analogy. Analogies were used by Socrates (e.g. comparing what he did to the task of a midwife) or Plato (e.g. comparing the parts of the soul to a charioteer handling a black and a white horse). Although the use of analogies was common in former times it was regarded with suspicion by modern positivist philosophy (Inciarte 1973). Only recently has the use of analogies become a focal point of interest, since it was recognized as an important way of thinking by the cognitive sciences (cf. Thagard 1999, pp. 101-120).

When people argue they sometimes turn to analogies to clarify or support a point they are making. 'Analogies are resemblances between things of different types (...). In many cases the resemblance is not spelled out but left implicit.' (Shaw 1997, p. 167) Leonard Nelson, for example, starts his famous speech about the Socratic method with a comparison to playing a violin. In his case Nelson is emphasizing the need of acting instead of just talking about the action. But without further ado, both actions are also compared in virtue of their both being an art. A main advantage of this technique is the speaker being able to

---

6   Of course the media can manipulate what we see and believe, but manipulation can also happen if one is seeing something with one's own eyes. Being present is no guarantee it 'really' happened that way.

7   One person from the group asked: what about a participant in a SD being an expert on the topic in question?

use a comparison[8] without explicitly having to name the connotations coming into the head of the listener. A well known example is the reference to a crowded boat ('the boat is full') to show a land has no more capacity for refugees (cf. Kienpointner 1996, p. 177f.). A feminist (cf. Dworkin, MacKinnon 1993, p. 83) might want to point out something had to be done even if pornography[9] were only a symptom and not the cause of misogyny. For that reason she chooses high fever to emphasis the necessity of doing something to reduce the temperature. By choosing this example the listener is urged to see pornography in relation to disease without the speaker having to say it openly. Analogies do only work if the listener understands the analogy being used (see Hofstadter 1996, pp. 336f.). Sometimes it is even necessary to understand meta-analogies (see Hofstadter 1996, pp. 343f).

It may happen that somebody taking part in a SD chooses an analogy in his argumentation. I remember another SD on 'the limits of tolerance' where the boiling point of water was chosen to point out a change in status (from liquid to gas) to stress the limits for tolerance. The members of the group accepted the analogy that a certain 'boiling point' could be fixed. Both starting points for the analogies (fever, boiling water) are experiences the speaker has had himself and would therefore fulfil the criteria required for a SD. But would the use of these analogies be allowed as part of an argumentation inside a SD? The distinction between the content of the argument and its form is necessary at this point. Even if one is perfectly happy with the conclusion that the other person reaches, it might not be based upon sound argumentation.

People using arguments in a SD do not automatically argue differently compared to outside a SD. It would be rather interesting to find out if and how the facilitator (or any other participant) enforces the norms laid down for arguments in a SD. But one could ask whether it is really

---

8   Kienpointner distinguishes between comparisons and analogies (cf. Kienpointner 1996, pp. 103-116 for comparisons and 176-183 for analogies). An analogy — which for Kienpointner is an indirect comparison — compares things which are on the first sight incomparable, but reveal on closer inspection they are comparable in an essential aspect (cf. Kienpointner 1996, p. 176).

9   The feminist criticism of pornography is not new and took mainly place some years ago. The French films 'Romance' (Catherine Breillat) and 'Baise-moi' (Virginie Despentes and Coralie Thrinh Thi) restarted the discussion about women and pornography.

necessary to enforce these restrictions? If the restrictions were[10] strictly enforced some types of arguments would not be allowed inside a SD. If there should be restrictions on the types of arguments allowed in a SD, it will be essential to find out which arguments really could occur in a SD. It would be necessary to show very clearly why certain arguments should be excluded. Reference to the writings of Nelson and Heckmann seem simply to be arguments from authority. It could be worthwhile to bring the problems of authority into the open instead of simply banning the reference to authority from the SD altogether. If analogies are used in the SD it would pay to have a closer look at these sort of arguments to see their advantages and their disadvantages (cf. Shaw 1997, chapter 14). Even without research into the practice of argumentation in SD, it would be a good idea to focus more on the arguments and the argumentation to foster the positive effects of SD.

References

Bayer, Klaus (1999): Argument und Argumentation. Opladen.

Coyne, Anthony M. (1984): Introduction to Inductive Reasoning. London.

Dworkin, Andrea; MacKinnon, Catharine (1993): Questions and Answers. In: D. E. H. Russel (ed.): Making Violence Sexy — Feminist Views on Pornography. Buckingham, pp 78-96.

Edwards, Jane A. (ed.) (1993): Talking Data: Transcription and Coding in Discourse Research. Hillesdale.

Givón, Talmy (1995): Coherence in Text vs. Coherence in Mind. In: M. A. Gernsbacher and T. Givón (eds.): Coherence in Spontaneous Text. Amsterdam.

Heckmann, Gustav (1993): Das Sokratische Gespräch. Erfahrungen in philosophischen Hochschulseminaren. Mit einem Vorwort zur Neuausgabe von Dieter Krohn. Frankfurt.

Hofstadter, Douglas R. (and the Fluid Analogies Research Group) (1996): Die FARGonauten über Analogie und Kreativität. Stuttgart. (American original: Fluid Concepts and Creative Analogies, New York 1995).

---

10 How participants in a SD really argue has not been investigated. It seems to me from my limited experience that participants and facilitators sometimes ignore the strict rules without running into to trouble.

Inciarte, Fernando (1973): Eindeutigkeit und Variation. Freiburg, München.

Kienpointner, Manfred (1996): Vernünftig argumentieren. Reinbek.

Krohn, Dieter (2000): Welcome to the Conference and a Short Introduction to the Socratic Method. In: Conference Folder 3rd International Conference 'Socratic Dialogue and Ethics', pp. 3-5.

Neißer, Barbara (1989): Leonard Nelson's Sokratische Methode im Vergleich mit der Themenzentrierten Interaktion. In: D. Krohn et. al. (eds.): Das Sokratische Gespräch. Ein Symposion. Hamburg, pp. 25-45.

Raupach-Strey, Gisela (1989): Werkstatt-Reflexionen aus Leiterin-Perspektive zu einem unvollendeten Sokratischen Gespräch. In: Zeitschrift für Didaktik der Philosophie, pp. 32-42.

Roß, Klaus (1996): Zum Teufel mit dem advocatus diaboli? In: D. Krohn; B. Neißer; W. Nora (eds.): Diskurstheorie und Sokratisches Gespräch. Schriftenreihe der Philosophisch-Politischen Akademie. Vol. III. Frankfurt, pp. 165-173.

Shaw, Patrick (1997): Logic and its Limits. 2nd edition. Oxford.

Thagard, Paul (1999): Kognitionswissenschaft. Stuttgart (American original: Mind: Introduction to Cognitive Science, Cambridge, Mass.; London 1996)

Horst Gronke

First things first!
Analytic and strategic phases in Socratic Dialogue

1. The four "companions" of Socratic Dialogue [SD]

If nowadays we go away somewhere, then we usually know the destination of the journey. We start in A and arrive in B. This was not always so. When, at the beginning of the 19th century, Alexander von Humboldt started his famous research expedition to the jungle area of South and Central America, he moved in an unknown area. It wasn't easy for him and his companions to attain a realistic idea of what would await them. You couldn't send out an aeroplane or satellite to find out about the area in advance. This wouldn't even have been desirable. In the end, it was all about finding and investigating something new. After all, Humboldt's experiences and his immense understanding of what was then common knowledge helped him to get used to the unknown. In addition, he didn't simply go 'into the blue'. He proceeded systematically. He considered his next steps well. On such a dangerous journey it was important to use the strengths and the time effectively, that is, to take first things first.

In a certain way, this is similar to Socratic dialogue [SD]. An SD is comparable to an adventure trip. It is all about an unusual kind of speaking to each other, different from that which we are used to in everyday life. The dialogue partners enter unknown territory. You cannot know in advance what will come out as a result at the end. Yes, it can be that one takes long detours. It can even happen that one doesn't obtain any satisfactory 'result' at all.

Humboldt's expedition lasted a long time, some years. The SD lasts a long time too — in comparison with the short conversations we are used to in everyday life and in our jobs. A Socratic colleague advised me some years ago to devote as much time as necessary to the dialogue. He thought: Socratics have time. In my opinion one should do exactly the reverse. If an important topic needs more time to be cleared, then it is important to handle the time particularly effectively. One doesn't take detours voluntarily. Taking time must not mean wasting time. In addition, SDs are also about achieving as good as possible a result in as short as possible a space of time. Of course, it should be a result, and a journey to the result, which corresponds to the Socratic method. The special challenge is the combination of effectiveness and methodological discipline.

In a Socratic content dialogue, the participants discuss the correct understanding and validity of opinions and judgements. During the dialogue a Socratic facilitator takes care that the participants keep to the point, refer to each other, think in relation to experience, look for an answer worthy of a consensus, formulate and validate the more abstract assumptions, etc. But, even if all these things are seriously considered by the participants, a Socratic content dialogue can still get into trouble. Essentially, this undesired result can have four different causes.

a) There are *problems in the personal and interpersonal dimension.* Some participants feel disturbed by the behaviour of other participants. One of the participants doesn't dare to speak in the group. Another participant simply doesn't manage to calm his frustration with the views that are stated by his dialogue partners, etc. These problems can become subjects of a so-called *meta-dialogue.* [1]

b) There are *methodological problems.* As the Socratic method is unusual, it can result in a lack of understanding in the dialogue again and again. For example, some participants ask: How does one ask for presuppositions of understanding and validity? What is the role of agreement in the SD? Why avoid hypothetical examples? Why put sentences in concrete terms? Why not start with conceptual definitions? Why formulate complete sentences? Why visualise the

---

1   This is the name which Gustav Heckmann, the mentor of the Socratic method after the second World War, has given this type of dialogue. One could use "meta-dialogue", in contrast to Heckmann, also as a primary concept for all forms of the conversation which are outside the content argumentation. I hold on to the traditional use of "meta-dialogue". As an umbrella term for all types of dialogue outside the content argumentation I suggest: "accompanying dialogues".

course of dialogue? These and similar questions must be settled in such a way that the participants don't lose their enthusiasm for active participation in the dialogue by straining their patience. *The methodology dialogue* has an informative and — if reasons for a methodological measure are required — argumentative character.

c) There are *problems in seeing the point of the discussion*, in understanding the relevance of the expressed thoughts and the way the argumentation has proceeded. These problems can be clarified by *analysing the content dialogue (phases of analysis)*.

d) There are *problems in deciding the way the argumentation should proceed*, in deciding which points should be discussed next. These problems can be discussed in *strategy phases*.

These four phases accompanying the content dialogue, the "companions" of the SD, react to the challenges coming out from the inside of a Socratic content dialogue. They don't form any outer net which is put artificially on it. They offer the dialogue partners the possibility of organising their dialogue independently.

Figure 1: The four "companions" of Socratic Dialogue [accompanying dialogues]

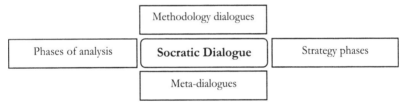

I leave questions regarding the design of the meta-dialogue aside in this essay.[2] I pay particular attention to the analysis and strategy phases. The design of these phases depends fundamentally on the methodological aspects of Socratic argumentation. I will therefore explain the central aspects of Socratic argumentation first.

---

2 Clarifications of the main object of the meta-dialogue, namely with regard to the feelings which can hinder or promote the argumentative dialogue, I have made together with Lily Sparnaay in: Gronke/Sparnaay 2004.

2. Socratic argumentation: methodological basics

The aim of a neo-Socratic content dialogue consists in communication about those criteria, scales, values and principles on which sensible judgement and decision-making are based (regressive abstraction). This way is provided by a characteristically *Socratic question looking for a more general knowledge related to a type of situation (2nd order question) or a completely general knowledge (3rd order question)*. Fundamental principles and basic orientations are worked out on the basis of generally comprehensible situations of experience (example situations). They form the basis of understanding for discourses orientated at the individual cases.[3]

The Socratic method is indicated *by another four main aspects* besides the Socratic question and the way of argumentation provided by it:

- *autonomy* (thinking for oneself),
- *co-operation* (thinking together),
- *referring to experience* (thinking specific),
- *searching for truth* (thinking by reasons).

These are general criteria and orientations. What does the philosophical argumentation look like in concrete, however? Put differently: How can one come closer to the truth in an argumentation in which nobody has the power to decide between true and wrong reasons? How can one know whether one comes closer to the truth if one doesn't already know the truth? Is there a method for finding the way in an unknown area?

One obtains more than a clue from Aristotle's conception of a practical argumentation. He had developed it in his *Nicomachean Ethics*. Aristotle determines moral prudence as an interplay of the internalised knowledge of the common good ways of behaviour in society (ethical virtue) with knowledge of the concrete circumstances. The *morally prudent person* knows how one applies a virtuous attitude (as an internalisation of a system of norms and values) to the specific case. Aristotle's method of coming to justified behaviour in the individual case is described as a *practical syllogism*. Its basis is a general action orientation (norm, value). This is connected with the distinctive feature of a situation or fact. The action decision then results from it. A practical syllogism could, for example, look like this:

---

3   See the two essays of Kopfwerk Berlin 2004 on the methodology of the SD.

- If one should help all people living in poverty (general premise)
- and this person lives in poverty (concrete premise),
→ then the one who is capable of it should help this person (concluding action).

However, one may not read the model of the practical syllogism deductively. On the one hand, it is difficult in many cases to apply general norms or values clearly to a situation or a feature of it. On the other hand, it is frequently controversial whether and in which regards the general norm or value is valid.

Therefore, Aristotle designed a more comprehensive and more fundamental model of justification, in which he integrated the practical syllogism: the *stadium model*.

> "Let us not fail to notice, however, that there is a difference between arguments from and those to the first principles. For Plato, too, was right in raising this question and asking, as he used to do, 'Are we on the way from or to the first principles?' There is a difference, as there is in a race-course between the course from the judges to the turning-point and the way back. For, while we must begin with what is evident, things are evident in two ways – some to us, some without qualification. Presumably, then, we must begin with things evident to us." (Aristotle, Nicomachean Ethics, 1095 a 31–b 4)

Aristotle uses the picture of the Olympic double racecourse with a start in the west around a turning point and return to the starting line. With this picture he illustrates his model of reflective practical argumentation, the so-called *Epagogé*.

Figure 2: The stadium model

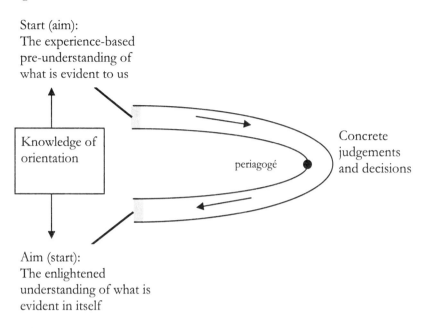

Start (aim):
The experience-based
pre-understanding of
what is evident to us

Knowledge of
orientation

periagogé

Concrete
judgements
and decisions

Aim (start):
The enlightened
understanding of what is
evident in itself

The arguing shall proceed just like the runner in the double racecourse. This one runs from the starting line to the turning point and back again to the starting point. The arguing one whose argumentation aims at a judgement or an action starts on a level on which a quantity of knowledge already is evident to him (due to education, tradition, culture). (Start). That is, we always know how to judge and act in specific situations (and we do that daily) although we often have this knowledge only as a tacit knowledge, as a situation-related pre-understanding of our basic action orientations (principles).

In order to find the principles out in a reflexive attitude (attitude of the periagogé as a reversal of thinking), we can reconstruct the way of the practical syllogism to our concrete judgements or actions (turning point). We clarify what was already somehow evident to us before (pre-understanding). We bring to light, at the same time, what of this "evidence for us" earns the title of an "evidence-in-itself". The "evidence-in-itself" is the generally valid principles embodied in the virtuous attitudes. There will constantly remain a need for clarification with this. Therefore we must start the "stadium race" (pre-understanding → judgement/action → understanding) once more, although now from a more enlightened pre-understanding. Reflective practical argumentation has a circular structure, the structure of a *hermeneutical spiral*. This means for the SD:

- Starting with concrete experience (example situation).
- Formulating of specific judgements in starting out from an implicit knowledge of principles.
- Going back from the specific judgements to the general presuppositions backing them.
- Correction of the judgement with respect to the example situation on the basis of the knowledge of the principles brought to light before.

One can find many moves of argumentation of this sort in Plato's SDs. The dialogue *Laches* delivers a prime example for the Socratic way of argumentation (Laches, 189 d–193 d). In the dialogue about the right education art it is all about the virtues to be learned, particularly bravery. Socrates is not allowed to give examples as an answer ("if anyone is willing, keeping in his rank, to oppose the enemy, and does not fly, I well know that he will be a brave man."(Laches, 190 e)). It is for him all about a generally valid determination, a principle which applies to all situations, not only for specific situations, e.g. war situations. Reasons, not examples, must be given.

Because such an examination must unavoidably start out from the concrete lifeworld (what is "evident to us") this is a difficult task. Socrates responds to this challenge of a radical periagogé or a reflexive change of attitude by a special method, the *elenctic hypothesis method* (Politeia, 514 a–518 b). Plato illustrated this method in the allegory of the cave. According to this method, at first *a hypothesis* is put forward. This hypothesis must not be any hypothesis you like, but a hypothesis which is constitutive, that means indispensable, for the self-understanding of one's own life and professional practice. In the next step Socrates secures — if necessary — the actual, well-considered *acceptance of this hypothesis by the dialogue partner*, e.g. with questions such as "Did you think through this well?" "Are you really sure?" "Is this your real opinion?" etc. Finally, there is check to see *whether the logical conclusions from these hypotheses are coherent with other hypotheses or conclusions from them* being similarly deeply rooted in one's life. If a contradiction arises, the examination must be taken once more with changed hypotheses. So the facilitator must reflect upon which general opinions are seriously accepted by all participants in the previous argumentation even if the participants in a SD are not able to make them explicit.

Figure 3: The elenctic hypothesis method of Socrates

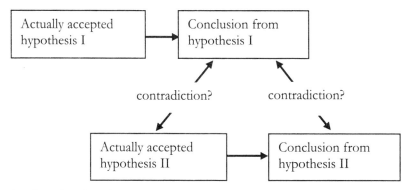

So that the thread isn't lost in such a common justification dialogue according to the hypothesis method with its exchange of pros and cons, the relation to the previous statements must be clarified again and again. The Socratic *elenctics* (Greek: justification by refutation) is not only future-oriented, it is fundamentally an art of memory. Socrates explains this to his dialogue partner Eutyphron in the Platonic dialogue of the same name. He responds there to the common reproach he would twist people's words like Daidalos, the master builder of the labyrinth of Minotaurus, instead of helping them out of the wrong track:

> "Asserting these things, can you wonder that your discourse does not appear to be fixed, but wandering? And can you accuse me as being the Daedalus that causes them to wander, when you yourself far surpass Daedalus in art, and make your assertions to revolve in a circle? Or do you not perceive that our discourse, revolving again, comes to the same? For you remember that in the former part of our discourse, the holy, and the dear to divinity, did not appear to us to be the same, but different from each other: or do you not remember?"(Plato, Eutyphron, 15 b-c)

Argumentation has already always been intersubjectively oriented. Argumentation wants *to convince*. Argumentation is aimed *at consensus according to an agreement with each other, not at consensus according to taking over another opinion*. On the other hand, a *disagreement* is an indispensable presupposition for argumentation. Argumentation is pointless without disagreement. So argumentation is an *interplay of disagreement and agreement*. How can dialogue partners come from a disagreement to an agreement, however?

We try to change a dissent to a consent by relating to assumptions belonging to the unproblematic (consensual) part of the dialogue partners' arguments. A dialogue in which the participants extend their doubts and distrust to everything and everybody can never be successful. A consensus-oriented argumentation has a *dissent-consent-consent-structure*.

In order to reach a possible consensus, look within the dissent for the assumptions which all dialogue partners share! So a Socratic rule of argumentation could be.

Figure 4: The dissent-consent-consent-structure of argumentation

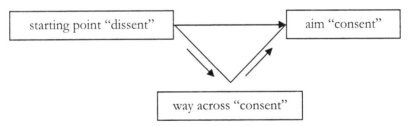

Foundation means *justification* (to others). Therefore foundation cannot find the grounds of the validity in putatively first axioms or last reasons which are independent of communication. Foundation must be based on the common convictions of a communication community. The function of a model is to perform this kind of reasoning in an organised way.

The reference point of an assertion/a judgement is a concrete situation. Therefore the argumentation, that is, the examination of an assertion, starts with analysing the concrete situation. The central information which arises from it represents the *reason/ground* for the assertion in an argumentation. Many types of argumentation take this course in everyday life.

What usually remains unnamed in everyday considerations are the *general assumptions*. They make the logically plausible *transition* from the features of the situation to the judgements comprehensible and acceptable. These *resources of consensus for the argumentative clarification of a disagreement must have the implicit form of a rule of inference* to be effective in the argumentation process (if situations of the type A, then judgements of the type B). If the rules of inference become problematic themselves, one must go to a still deeper level. One then goes to the basic principles to which a universal validity claim is connected. In the SD it is all about *general reasons in the form of rules of inference or principles*.

Figure 5: The structure of the argumentation

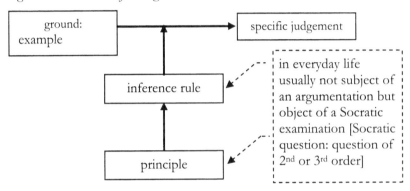

This model offers an open basis for the analysis of argumentation. By the help of it one can easily determine the five *targets of an argumentation*.

(1)   If there is a disagreement concerning the specific judgement, at first one will check *whether the judgement is formulated precisely*. This is an important step in the SD. An imprecise wording of the judgement can impair the whole subsequent examination.

(2)   One then will check whether the *features of the situation (the reasons)* are correctly understood.

(3)   One then will check the *validity of the rule of inference*.

(4)   Another step consists in controlling the logical correctness of the *transition from the rule of inference to the concrete judgement*.

In the case of a dissensus on the validity of the rule of inference one shall look for a more general indisputable assumption which can support it. If in turn this has the form of a rule of inference, the tests repeat according to step (3) and (4). If it has the form of a *principle* and if grave doubts appear then it is necessary to examine the validity of this principle.

3. Analytic and strategic phases in Socratic dialogue

If one is equipped with this methodological knowledge: What does this mean for the facilitation of a Socratic dialogue and for the orientation of the SD? Firstly, it means that the Socratic facilitator can give the participants information about the methodical features of the SD. But this is not the primary benefit of methodical know-how. It rather matters more to use this for the benefit of the concrete conducting of an SD.

The professional conducting of an SD is a difficult affair. It is especially because an SD must be conducted in an indirect manner, that the facilitator must be aware of as many aspects of the communication as possible.

A very significant aspect is moving forward as a group, moving together, making a common inquiry. Therefore the facilitator must be aware of what is to be achieved by the group in the course of argumentation. The facilitator should know what questions and what thoughts have been how intensively discussed, which conclusions are drawn from which premises, whether all participants have interpreted the argumentation in the same way, what has been excluded from the argumentation, etc.

In short, the facilitator must be aware of the *process*, the *structure* and the *logic* of the prior argumentation. While the methodological dialogue and the meta-dialogue are systematically distinguished from the content dialogue, the *analysis and strategy phases are in direct* connection with the content dialogue. They are genuine *parts* of the content dialogue. Two needs of clarification regularly appear, namely, in the internal context of argumentation.

At which point of the argumentation are we exactly? On which question are we working at the moment? Who can recapitulate how we have reached the present stage of the argumentation? What results have we reached during the previous course of dialogue? These are questions that are to be clarified in a phase of analysis, in a retrospective of the *structure, the process and the logic of the argumentation,* I propose.

How do we want to carry on? In which direction should our examination go? What are the most important sub-questions which we should answer? These are all questions about the specification of future steps of argumentation, which are addressed in a *strategy phase.*

In *strategy phases* it is decided whether the dialogue will take a productive course. Gustav Heckmann takes hold of them as the "sixth educational measure" under the idea of "conducting".

> "Measure six deals with those interventions by means of which the facilitator steers the dialogue in fruitful directions. By using these measures as well as focusing the dialogue on the current question [...] the facilitator protects the dialogue from the fate of many unguided discussions, including the loss of a clear train of thought, and of the dialogue running into the sand. [...] To me (G. Heckmann) the sixth measure makes the greatest demands on the facilitator – to recognise and to use fruitful starting points and questions." (Heckmann 2004, pp. 112 ff.)

It is a difficult enterprise to make strategy decisions within a group sensibly. It therefore isn't surprising that strategy phases, particularly, can paralyse a dialogue; they frequently are the cause of meta-dialogues. What are the criteria that are used by a group to fix the next step? How and when does one end strategy dialogues best? What influence does the facilitator exert on the decision?

Admittedly, no professional measure will guarantee a completely compelling course of argumentation. Pre-assumptions flow into every argumentation unexplained and unchecked. One wonders, therefore, to what extent one can *count* on the unsteady ground of a more or less clear pre-understanding to reach fairly sensible decisions on the course of the dialogue? Most strategic decisions in an SD are done in secret, in the course of argumentation. The participants are then not aware of the strategy situation. Either they take up a suggestion of the facilitator or that of another participant. They don't think much about it. Such a procedure is susceptible to a lasting confusion.

I have noticed that among others the following precede *well-considered* strategy decisions: Where do we actually stand? What was the starting point of our argumentation? Which questions have we already settled? What have we resolved to do (in earlier strategy decisions)? Have we failed to see something? Strategy dialogues presuppose a relatively clear understanding of the past argumentation as a solid starting basis. The phase of analysis is all about remembering the shared understanding and clearing the argumentation of misunderstandings. If there is misunderstanding, vagueness, non-transparency, then the dialogue will be negatively influenced. Here, I introduce a model which includes the analytic elements as comprehensively as possible.

3.1 Analytic phases: the "dialogram"

The phase of analysis *accompanies* the content argumentation. In it the dialogue partners are arguing *not on the content but on the former content argumentation*. As a matter of fact, this is a usual procedure in an SD: if the facilitator or a participant summarises what was discussed till now. These summaries are of a delicate nature. They can be incomplete or miss the topic completely in essential points. It is methodically more reliable to do the recapitulation of the course of argumentation with the guide of a practicable model. This can prove to be useful both for the reflections of the Socratic facilitator before and after the dialogue and for the communication of the dialogue partners with each other. In a phase of analysis, the reason (of the participants) can show itself as transparent, coherent and logical without professionalised logic know-how having to be taken up. Through this a reflexive self-confidence in reason grows.

This self-confidence is, admittedly, bound to perception (Anschauung). "Abstract" analysing dialogues, in the sense of a *course* in the logic of argumentation, are not a sufficient preparation for the use of reason in special situations in life. For analysing an SD the facilitator can use methods of visualising. I have experimented with such models for some years. There are methods which are regularly used for the analyse of scientific or technical texts, for example, flow charts. In my SDs I tested a method that is more specific for the challenges of a SD, for its character of communication and dialogue. The name of this method could be a "Dialogram" (Dialogue + Diagram). It is a combination of different techniques of visualising and analysing (of linear and network-procedures), completed by some elements that are related to the specific method of argumentation in an SD.

Besides, the Dialogram has the advantage that one can make, by means of it, an analysing dialogue with the whole group. Especially for ambitious groups it is important that the participants not only train their

172

ability to think together but are also able to reflect (and if need be to correct) the process of common thinking. After an analysing dialogue the participants have a better knowledge of which questions they have answered, which questions are not sufficiently discussed, which theses are related to which questions, which conclusions they have drawn from which assumptions, etc.

The model shall be able to show the multi-dimensional relations between speakers, listeners and propositions schematically. If one bases this on the canon of *rhetoric, dialectic and logic formulated by Aristotle, a corresponding three level model* arises:

a) rhetorical level in the speaker-listener relation,
b) dialectical level in the speaker-proposition relation,
c) logical level in the proposition-proposition relation.

This division after the classic disciplines of the Trivium of the artes liberales has contained a more modern version. Jürgen Habermas also has suggested a trinomial subdivision of the types of argumentation. He distinguishes between the three analytic aspects of the argumentation as a *process, as a procedure and as a product* (cf. Habermas 1981, pp. 47 ff.).

-   According to the *process*, it is all about arranging the communication between the dialogue partners to be *as ideal as possible*. It is all about the best possible mutual understanding and thinking with each other with equal rights. Only the force of the better argument shall get somewhere, any influences disturbing dialogue partners are to be avoided. The question is: How well do the dialogue partners pay attention to each other?

-   According to the *procedure* it is all about designing the course of the argumentation appropriately. To obtain an *agreement* of high quality, the problematic validity claims about propositions must be checked by the dialogue partners. The question is: How coherently do the individual steps of argumentation refer to each other?

-   According to the *product* it is all about producing arguments which are logically consistent. Conclusions and premises must provide *truth*. The question is: Is the argument valid?

The visual arranging of this scheme must correspond to the step-by-step procedures which are characteristic of neo-Socratic dialogues. This doesn't play an essential role, however, on the *level of production* of the individual steps of argumentation. Arguments can be represented and analysed in the lower writing area (see dialogram) *sequentially* by means of suitable models of argumentation (e.g. the ones described above).

The marking of the upper writing area provided for the *level of process* doesn't make any particular demands on competence in visualisation either. Here it is all about recording in short notes the interpersonal occurrences which have restrictingly or beneficially had an essential effect on the course of the dialogue: the influence of the facilitator on the course of argumentation and the interpersonal situation of communication or observations of the relationship of the participants of the group with each other (e.g., "last hour: only 3 of 10 participants involved in the dialogue"). In order to show the interpersonal relationships of the participants with each other, their roles as dialogue partners and the dynamic structure of the group as a "system" graphically, the method of sociometry developed by Jacob Levy Moreno offers its services (cf. Moreno 1934). The procedure of illustration *of the sociogram* allows us to clarify the complete structure of positive and negative connections between the members of the group (cohesion of the group) under the points of view of the mutual ascription of expert knowledge, of mutual liking and of mutual respect.

The visualisation of the *procedural level* forming the core area of the dialogram is more demanding. Here it is all about illustrating on the time axis the *structure of the course of argumentation* with its interplay between questions, sub-questions, descriptions, explanations of concepts, judgements, doubts, pros and cons, etc. in their relational connection. There are attempts to use the model of the *flow chart* for this visualizing analysis. The main problems of this model are the relative inflexibility and the restricted ability to show the logical relations between the remarks in their dynamics. As a matter of fact the flow chart doesn't go fundamentally further than what is formulated in words on a blackboard or a flipchart. The so-called *Mind Mapping* method of Tony Buzan (cf. Buzan 1996) would be more adequate in this regard, but it is primarily put together for creating ordered ideas and doesn't do justice to the qualitatively heavy demand which is made in an analysis.

Network technology can meet the requirements of a procedurally oriented analysing dialogue most appropriately in my opinion. It shows particularly the advantage that the relationships between the single sentences and the respective functions of the sentences could be marked clearly. Already with a little list of ascriptions of the functions almost the complete logical structure of logical relations of a SD can be included. A presupposition is that the participants' remarks recorded on the blackboard in the course of a SD are numbered ongoingly. The numbers then can be written down on the scheme instead of the sentences. The Socratic initial question gets the number 0. I suggest for the identification of the functions of the sentences:

"**I**" for an information statement,
"**!**" for judgement, thesis, assertion,
"**?**" for a question,
"**s**" for the situation-related character of a remark,
"**g**" for the general character of a remark,
"**C**" for a consensual statement.

Further labels can be added any time if necessary (thriftily, however, otherwise it will become confusing!) The relationships between the sentences marked by arrows should be abbreviated, e.g. "X answers to Y", "central concept", "X justifies Y", "under the condition of", etc. The rule of notation is: always refer to the sentence at which the arrow points.

For the initial stage of a SD (see the sentences quoted below) the dialogram represented on the following page could give an illustration.

Flipchart writing of a SD:

[0]   **How selfish may voluntary engagement be?**

[1 a]   Example: "third world charity shop: I earn money by working in a third world charity shop."

[1 b] Example: "Christmas surplus: I took the sweets which couldn't be distributed for my own use, however, I collected the whole amount of the refund."

[1 c] Example: "distribution of rooms: I organised the distribution of the rooms. I assigned a single room to myself."

[2 a] Why did you take the surplus of sweets?

[2 b] Why didn't you want to give the money back?

[2 c] Were you allowed to keep the surplus?

[3] I was allowed to keep the surplus of sweets because I had made a good buy.

[4] It required a lot of energy and time from me to find a good buy.

[5] I was allowed to keep the surplus of sweets without giving the money back for the purchase of the sweets because I made a lot of effort to purchase cheap products.

[6 a] One who acts charitably earns the right of the fulfilment of one's own needs.

[6 b] If a person does something for others and the effort is great, then he may receive something of this, too. (Consensus)

Figure 7: Dialogram according to the starting phase of a SD

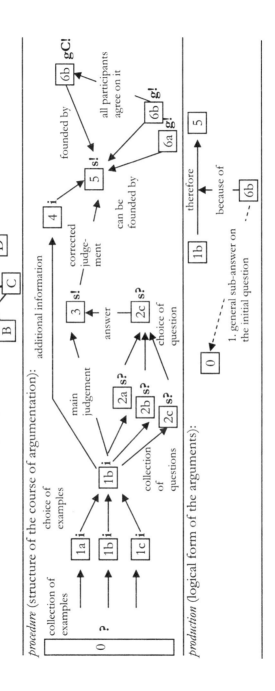

3.2 Strategy phases

There are good preconditions for the following phase of dialogue if the analysis of the course of dialogue has been successful and if all participants know how the previous argumentation has gone. Through this, however, the group isn't released from having to make decisions for the further course of the dialogue.

Sometimes the participants have the feeling that the discussion doesn't come to a conclusion, that they don't find a convincing method of argumentation, that they cannot move beyond a difficulty in the argumentation. In short, people don't know how to proceed. What should be done? Should they clarify judgement A, discuss question B, concentrate on doubt C, take up idea D, examine argument F, etc.? What method should be used to decide the next steps of argumentation? Which criteria are useful in finding reasonable strategic decisions?[4]

These phases are delicate situations in the SD. One should not leave their mastering to destiny. One should handle them in a considerate way. The question is: How can we arrive at strategy decisions? There are *two ways:*

The way of Socrates

The participants could delegate the proposals or decisions for the proceeding of the argumentation to the facilitator. In this respect the facilitator behaves like a facilitator on the level of content argumentation, but on the strategic level he behaves like a *leader.* Then he or she tells the others where they have to go. He decides which idea is fruitful for the dialogue, which opinions should be discussed, and what can be left. This corresponds approximately to the behaviour of Socrates in Plato's dialogues when he steers the dialogue with his questions in a certain direction.

Because in every SD there is not enough time to discuss all ideas, and because the patience of the participants and their ability to concentrate are limited, this leading behaviour of a Socratic facilitator is necessary, a necessary evil, so to speak. The idea of a discourse completely free of domination is a fiction (though helpful as a regulative idea). It depends

---

4   On this subject see also the essays of Brune/Mostert 2004 and Ross 2004.

on the amount of time, the members of the group, the complexity of the theme and on other conditions how strong or how weak this leading behaviour should be. The rule of thumb is: *As little steering as possible, as much steering as necessary!*

A good facilitation of a SD is characterised, not just by the competence of the facilitator to initiate a fertile dialogue situation, but by the strategic orientation that the Socratic facilitator gives to the dialogue by his or her interventions. It is therefore a special art of the Socratic facilitation to ask the right questions in the right place in the dialogue. This art is, for example, particularly important in dialogues in professional contexts where it is important to produce good results in a very short time.

Sometimes the participants of a SD speak about the future proceeding of the argumentation and about possible next steps but don't make an explicit distinction between the strategic and content dialogues. In a way that is absolutely correct, due to the fact that content argumentation is interwoven with strategic argumentation. In these situations the facilitator has the task of recognising strategic phases of the dialogue as strategic phases, of identifying the essential strategic elements, of taking care of the reasonable decision, which should not be based on prejudice and power.

The participants' way

Another, more difficult and time-consuming way to clarify questions of the argumentation strategy is that the group themselves decide – in a *strategy dialogue*. In it the Socratic facilitator takes the role of a facilitator (not of a leader). The question is then: How should strategy dialogues be conducted? What is different to the facilitation of a content dialogue?

The most essential difference to pay attention to is that the group must come to a decision in a relatively short time. Strategy dialogues are decision dialogues. In contrast, the content argumentation doesn't end in a decision but either in a consent or in a dissent. It would be a category mistake to decide about the truth or untruth of a judgement. In content dialogues you can try to discover the truth; in strategy dialogues you can plan the route of the argumentation journey. This doesn't mean that strategy dialogues are to be characterised as instrumental and that the reference to the truth would be unimportant. Although strategy dialogues can serve any purpose (e.g. the purpose to win power and advantages over other people), in SDs they are always obliged to the communicative character of the argumentation. The strategy dialogue mustn't be led by the putting across of one's own opinion but by the search for truth. In an SD it is all about the route you think of as the best for the discovery of truth.

This starts with the choice of an example situation, by means of it the Socratic question shall be discussed, it continues with the specification of sub-questions, and leads up to fundamental decisions on the course of the dialogue.

Sometimes the group are aware that there is a serious problem with proceeding. In these cases it would be helpful to interrupt the content argumentation and to start with a *separate strategy dialogue*. Then the facilitator must give the methodological frame for the strategy dialogue and pay attention to the participants' following the rules for a strategy dialogue.

The strategy dialogue

In this essay I want to work out (by means of concrete material I collected in a workshop offered together with my colleague Willem Laan at the Loccum conference) what are the most important strategic elements in a SD, how a strategy dialogue is to be initiated, conducted and finished, which methodological orientations can be given, which criteria are important for reasonable decisions about the direction of argumentation, what the conditions are for the successful progress of strategic dialogue.

a) At first it is important to become aware of what the use *of the strategy dialogue* actually is. I see *three main aspects of benefit*:
   - *Transparency of the content dialogue:* By thinking about possible directions for the argumentation and the considered decision for one way, participants can make sense of the sensible course of the content dialogue. Reason keeps itself, so to speak, in its own hands.
   - *Time-saving:* By the well-considered design of the course of argumentation the danger of fruitless detours in the argumentation is reduced. The time available is used optimally.

- *Teamwork, shared responsibility:* By the common decisions on the further course of the dialogue, the group take on responsibility for their dialogue. They co-operate to find – according to the discussed subject – the best and, for all participants, most acceptable way of argumentation.

b) *When should a strategy dialogue (B) take place?*

It is best if a declared strategy dialogue doesn't become necessary. It is a sign of the success of a SD if strategy decisions are reached in connection with the progress of the content argumentation. Of course, the more the dialogue develops naturally, the better the group is in flow. In contrast: the more strategy dialogues become necessary, the more discordantly the group works. Sometimes, in particularly discordant groups, it can even happen that the strategy dialogue overrides the content dialogue completely. Therefore this rule is valid: Try to design the dialogue so that strategy dialogues need to be held as little as possible! Sometimes a strategy dialogue makes sense, however. There are three reasons for it essentially:

- It becomes necessary to choose between several alternatives in a sensible way, e.g. between the examination of several sub-questions.
- It consists in the group or one or more participants being vague about how to go further.
- The facilitator of the dialogue fears that the way chosen by the group will result in a dead end.

c) *How is a strategy dialogue argued?*

Above all, there are three kinds of arguments, arguments which are related to the *content,* arguments related to the Socratic *method* (see above chap. 2*),* and arguments related to the empirical *conditions* of dialogue.

With the arguments being related to the content it is important that the respective state of the argumentation is taken into consideration, eventually by an analysing dialogue (see chap. 3.1). If the confusion of one or several participants causes the strategy dialogue, the exact reason for the confusion should be cleared first. The next steps must tie appropriately to the steps before. Frequently the next steps also arise from the logic of the content, e.g. if we want to clarify X, we must first clarify Y.

Furthermore, suggestions for the strategy always already contain an anticipation of the future. One already has an approximate idea of which results the dialogue could lead to. (Humboldt also had an approximate idea of how things looked in the unknown South American jungle before he began his journey.) Such an anticipation is, on the one hand, helpful because it brings our intuition into play; on the other hand, it can tie us down to a suspected result too much. To avoid the latter, strategy decisions shouldn't be taken too narrowly and should be open to change. The distinction between short-term and long-term strategy decisions has proved its worth, too. It is valid that short-term strategy decisions are more obligatory than long-term. Long-term strategy decisions are more meaningful than short-term.

Arguments related to the Socratic method are primarily about the way of argumentation going the way of the regressive abstraction. The connection to the initial question has to be kept. The argumentation shall keep the reference to the concrete experience. A sub-question shall be examined until it is cleared satisfactorily for all involved.

With the arguments related to the conditions of dialogue it is primarily all about the consideration of the dynamics of the dialogue. If very heterogeneous ideas are discussed in a group, it makes pragmatically more sense to stick to small strategy steps and to orientate strictly around the selected example. The degree of complexity of the next steps should be determined in looking at the efficiency, the engagement and the time resources of the group. A dialogue is successful primarily when one finds the right rhythm which is adequate to the "system" of the SD group. In addition, primarily in professional contexts, the expectations of the participants play an important role for the regulation of the argumentation strategy.

d) *How does the group come to a decision?*
In contrast to the Socratic content dialogue, the purpose of the strategy dialogue is to make a decision. The argumentation in the strategy dialogue prepares the decision. The acceptance of the strategy decisions depends very much on all participants bringing in

and explaining their views with no important argument being passed over. As a rule, one will try to identify the decisive argument.

It has turned out, then, that strategy decisions are most likely to be accepted if the decisions arise from the trend of the argumentation, if there is an agreement on the strategy. Only if this doesn't turn out well, should one use decision procedures (e.g. majority votes or the vote of the Socratic facilitator.) Although it should be taken into account that the minority at least does not regard the decision as totally absurd. The decision should have the support of all participants.

Strategy decisions threaten to fall quickly into oblivion. Therefore it is important to write down the decision additionally to the suggestions for the strategy and the respective arguments. Some Socratic facilitators fix a time frame at the beginning of the strategy dialogue. I am not convinced of this measure. It doesn't match the dynamics of an SD. I try, nonetheless, to concentrate the dialogue on the essential and to waste no time. A good means to prevent the getting out of hand of strategy dialogues is the rule that no argument may be reported repeatedly. The strict compliance with rules is by the way also a good means to prevent dissatisfaction with the strategy dialogue and prevent frustrating 'meta-dialogues' about strategy dialogues.

e) *What are the facilitator's tasks in the strategy dialogue?*
I have already pointed out that the role of the facilitator of the strategy dialogue isn't different from the role of the facilitator of the content dialogue in some respects. The facilitator makes clear that he or she is responsible for the characteristic Socratic course of the understanding process within the group: listening to each other, proceeding step by step, inquiring arguments, taking seriously all perspectives, being open to unusual solutions, etc. Also in the strategy dialogue the group is responsible for the course of the argumentation. The facilitator doesn't participate by their own contributions to the subject. He or she motivates the teamwork of the group, asks the participants for strategic proposals, asks for the arguments that back them and for agreements. As in the content dialogue the important contributions are written down.

But there are some tasks of the facilitator which are different either because they arise for the first time in the strategy dialogue or because they gain a stronger meaning in the strategy dialogue. A quite essential difference is that the facilitator of the strategy dialogue pushes to shorten it. Because in strategy dialogues the way to the unknown is discussed, they tend towards not finding any end. The facilitator must prevent this from happening. It also contributes to the brevity of the strategy dialogue if the facilitator summarises the course of the previous content dialogue concisely at the beginning of the strategy dialogue. The facilitator supports the participants in their decision-making primarily by measures which contribute to the clear arranging of their own thoughts: synthesizing and ordering proposals and arguments, using schemes or rough drawings to make the communication easier, reformulating proposals to make them more comprehensible.

The most significant difference is due to the decision process in a strategy dialogue. At the beginning of the strategy dialogue it is important that the facilitator explains its objective: to come to a decision in as short a time as possible. It is just as important to identify the strategy question considerably: What does it refer to? Is it put quite openly or does it start out from pre-formulated alternatives?

Perhaps the most important task in the strategy dialogue is to prepare and organise the decision procedure well. First of all, the facilitator makes the decision-making process clear (for example, one or two phases of argumentation, formulating clearly the proposals, choice by majority). He or she writes down the collected alternatives and — after the decision — the outcome. The facilitator could give the participants the following outline of the strategy phases:

Figure 8: The phases of strategy dialogue

initial stage [phase of understanding]	1. Cause (e.g. uncertainty of a participant concerning the course of dialogue) 2. Suggestion of a strategy dialogue 3. Look at the meaningfulness of a strategy dialogue 4. Clarification of the rules of a strategy dialogue
middle stage [phase of argumentation]	5. Collection of suggestions for the further procedure 6. Collection of arguments in support of the suggestions 7. Consideration of the arguments [search for the decisive argument]
final stage [phase of decision]	8. Implicit agreement about the decision procedures or explicit specification of the decision procedure 9. Decision 10. Explicit formulation of the decision

Sometimes, if the group cannot find a way to come to a decision the facilitator can influence the outcome of the decision, for example, by describing in his or her summary of the alternative ways the "good" alternatives more intensively. But the same is valid here as for the whole SD, namely the rule: *as much exertion of influence on the content as necessary, as little exertion of influence as possible!*

References

Aristotle (1980): The Nicomachean Ethics. Trans. by David Ross, revised by J. L. Ackrill and J. O. Urmson. Oxford University Press.

Brune, Jens Peter; Mostert, Pieter (2004): Strategische Maßnahmen und Strategiegespräch im Sokratischen Gespräch. In: D. Krohn; B. Neisser (eds.): Verständigung über Verständigung. Münster: Lit, pp. 63-87.

Buzan, Tony; Buzan, Barry (1996): The Mind Map Book: How to use Radiant Thinking to Maximize Your Brain's Untapped Potential. New York: E. P. Dutton/Plume.

Gronke, Horst; Sparnaay, Lily (2004): Feelings in a Socratic Dialogue on Feelings. In: P. Shipley; H. Mason (eds.): Ethics and Socratic Dialogue in Civic Society. Series on Socratic Philosophizing. Vol. XI, London/Münster: Lit, pp. 169-178.

Habermas, Jürgen (1984): The Theory of Communicative Action. Voume 1: Reason and the Rationalization of Society. Boston: Beacon Press.

Heckmann, Gustav (2004): Six pedagogical measures and Socratic Facilitation. In: R. Saran; B. Neisser (eds.): Enquiring Minds. Socratic Dialogue in Education. London: Trentham Books , pp. 107-120.

Kopfwerk Berlin (J. P. Brune et al.) (2004): The Methodology of Socratic Dialogue: Creating Socratic Questions and the Importance of Being Specific. In: P. Shipley; H. Mason (eds.): Ethics and Socratic Dialogue in Civic Society. Series on Socratic Philosophizing. Vol. XI, London/Münster: Lit, pp. 88-111.

Kopfwerk Berlin (J. P. Brune et al.) (2005): The Methodology of Socratic Dialogue: Regressive Abstraction — How to ask for and find philosophical knowledge. In: D. Krohn; J. P. Brune (eds.): Socratic Dialogue and Ethics. London/Münster: Lit, pp. 84-108.

Moreno, Jacob Levy (1934): Who Shall Survive? A New Approach to the Problems of Human Interrelations. Washington, D.C.: Nervous and Mental Disease Publishing Co.

Plato (1984): The Works of Plato. Ed. and trans. by Thomas Taylor. New York & London: Garland Publishing.

Ross, Klaus (2004): Wie geht es weiter? Entscheidungen für das Strategiegespräch. In: D. Krohn; B. Neisser (eds.): Verständigung über Verständigung. Münster: Lit, pp. 88-110.

Reports

Barbara Neisser/Rene Saran

How can Socratic Dialogue be used in Ethics Lessons in School?

This Workshop was attended by about a dozen people drawn from several countries. The majority were interested in the topic from the point of view of the role of the teacher. Thus, after covering Barbara's and Rene's Notes on 'Law and Practice' in Germany and Britain respectively, the group selected for discussion the question:

What does a teacher need to learn in order to be a successful Socratic facilitator?

In addressing this question, quite a few worries came to the surface concerning issues like inadequacy of teacher training and the challenges to teacher authority or to students' deeply held beliefs which Socratic Dialogue may provoke. These concerns are covered in later points of the discussion.

First some questions were asked:

How could teachers cope with the situation of having to provide (instead of Religious Education (RE)) alternative social and moral education, given the lack of training on the one hand, and the promise of such provision in some countries under new laws on the other? It was suggested that the Socratic Method could help teachers who had to teach alternative courses. Luxembourg was given as an example where new laws provided for children to withdraw from RE lessons in order to attend alternative social and moral education, but meanwhile teacher training had not ensured that enough teachers were qualified to staff such alternative provision.

So what are the difficulties in school for which Socratic facilitators need to be prepared if the introduction of Socratic Dialogue in their school is to be successful?

The discussion included the following points:

1. Introduction of Socratic Dialogue into a School

In the Workshop it became quite clear that in the Netherlands, Britain and Germany, for example, conditions were often favourable to introducing Socratic Dialogue. Relationships between students and staff were sufficiently relaxed and open for students and teachers to cope well with the challenge of participating in such a dialogue. In other countries, by contrast, where hierarchy in schools is still very entrenched, the situation was likely to be much more difficult. No one teacher alone can achieve the introduction of Socratic Dialogue. There must be a supportive environment.

Certainly regard has to be paid to the wider environment: the stage the school is at; how much support there is (or could be developed) for trying Socratic Dialogue with some groups of children; the multi-cultural nature of the school; the expectations and attitudes among parents and the local community; the trust among students and staff to ensure confidentiality is respected (for example, where a student openly shares a delicate situation).

2. Preparatory Steps

Children and students need to develop social skills, but the creation of opportunities for this should be part of a school's task anyway. To develop listening skills, tolerant attitudes and the ability to be articulate are all necessary for the success of a Socratic Dialogue, but are also valuable as future life skills. Schools and teachers can support children in developing these.

3. Timetable Issues

The normal school timetable decrees short lessons. For Socratic Dialogue longer periods are needed, like for example for group project work which is already a familiar practice in many secondary schools. Blocks of time over say 5-6 weeks could prove valuable. Rene's experience with secondary students is that half a school day (say a 4-hour morning with a half hour break) was as much as the students could manage on one day, because the concentration required to listen and participate exhausted them. Barbara said it also works well to have shorter periods (for example, a double lesson) twice a week. Group members could be expected for home work to keep a Socratic diary and the next lesson could then start with the reading aloud of one of the diaries or reports, to achieve continuity in the group's work.

4. The Age of the Children

Especially when working with younger children, some in the group saw it as important that the position of the teacher is not undermined. The teacher has the knowledge and is an authority. Introducing Socratic Dialogue might even be harmful in challenging teacher authority, making it difficult for the teacher to cope in the classroom and to maintain discipline (see next point).

5. Equality, not Hierarchy: the Teacher's Authority

As equality of all participants in a Socratic Dialogue is essential, this clearly would challenge the entrenched hierarchy existing in many schools for 50 or more years.

As facilitator, the teacher is still an authority — insisting on discipline and tolerance in the group. There is a difference between conducting a Socratic Dialogue with an adult group and one in a school. A school teacher has to manage the social behaviour of group members and ensure that conflicts between children are resolved in a tolerant manner, that is, that acceptance of different viewpoints prevails. What the teacher would not do is to give information or a 'package of knowledge'.

6. Independent Learning

In Socratic Dialogue, the children have to be guided by the teacher in their journey of independent self-discovery, and towards understanding. This is an unusual role for school, so often associated with conveying or teaching knowledge. Some saw a danger in developing student independence. A Socratic Dialogue might make students examine their basic beliefs and this could feel threatening to them.

It was asked whether the questions for a Socratic Dialogue need to be screened, effectively limiting topics. Some suggested it is best for children to formulate their questions together with their teacher.

Summary

Together, members of the workshop listed the following points at the end as an overview of their discussion:

- The usefulness of the Socratic Dialogue — it can be made to work in schools (some members still had reservations).
- The wider setting is of major importance in the successful introduction of Socratic Dialogue (school ethos, student/staff relationships, trust, openness, parental and community attitudes).
- Adequate teacher training and preparation is essential.
- Awareness that the teacher as facilitator is in a different situation from a facilitator of adult groups.
- Importance of selection of topic/question. Need for sensitivity and recognition that some topics may be unsuitable ("dangerous" was the word some used).
- Recognition that in a changing world students need to learn to be more autonomous, but also of the fact that different countries are at different stages in encouraging (or not, as yet) the development of independent learning by students.

Silke Pfeiffer

Ethics in Dialogue with Children

Philosophizing as Part of Today's Curriculum in Primary Schools in East Germany

Introdruction

In 1999, in the 'Land' of Mecklenburg-Vorpommern, in the northern part of East Germany, 'Philosophizing with Children' was introduced as a subject to replace religious education as part of the school curriculum.

The underlying idea was that children have lots of questions to ask and that philosophizing can help them to find answers and understand the world around them better.

The basic method of philosophizing as a form of teaching at school is dialogue. A dialogue can be started, for instance, by discussing questions such as 'why do all of us die one day?' Alternatively, stories, or other instructional materials, may serve to introduce children to philosophizing, or they can be involved in dialogue through role play.

Philosophizing with Children

In school this activity is mainly aimed at developing the ability to:

- formulate questions and ask further questions;
- reflect on a subject, discovering individual ways of thinking based on individual experiences;
- learn by reproducing the thoughts of others;
- participate in a dialogue;
- solve problems and cope with conflicts;
- learn in a multicultural environment (considering the values and traditions of other cultures).

As in any school subject we have to observe a certain structure within the subject of 'Philosophizing with Children'. To reflect the experiences of children, we have listed four items with reference to each of the four questions which were formulated by Immanuel Kant.

The Four Topics

What can I know?

Class 1: How can children discover, see, understand, and enjoy life?
Class 2: How does life grow and die?
Class 3: How can children be taught to ask questions and give answers?
Class 4: How can children be encouraged to pose additional questions and think about them?

What shall I do?

Class 1: Life in family and at school.
Class 2: Finding friends.
Class 3: The categories of good and bad.
Class 4: The categories of acting justly and unjustly.

What may I hope for?

Class 1: What do I expect others to do?
Class 2: Being happy.
Class 3: What do we believe in?
Class 4: Thinking about the future.

What is a human being?

Class 1: Who am I?
Class 2: Why am I different from others?
Class 3: How to live with others?
Class 4: Children in different cultures — in what respects are they alike, and how do they differ?

Socratic Dialogue as a Method in Primary School

I read a lot about Socratic Dialogue, and took part many a time as well. It seems to me that there is no uniform definition of what one has to understand by 'Socratic Dialogue'. What I am discussing here is the question: is it possible to conduct a Socratic Dialogue with primary school children? If yes, then certainly the dialogue will differ from one conducted with adults.

Below I present two examples of actual dialogues with primary-age children. Both variants in my view have four things in common with dialogues conducted with adults:

- The target of the dialogue is to get children to see a certain point;
- Children's concrete experience is the basis of any dialogue;
- Children are encouraged to formulate their own thoughts;
- Children compare their thoughts with those of other children.

The First Variant

This starts with a story by Berrie Heesen. Its title is 'Mary and Till Play Sparrow and Turtle'. The two children, while playing sparrow and turtle, come across the question 'who of the two animals is the wiser one?' and 'who is the faster one?'.

As a result the following discussion developed:

Peter: Shall we act that story, too?
Teacher: Which one of the two animals would you like to be?
Peter: The turtle!
Frank: That fits you, being the turtle.
            Peter: We could also take other animals, for instance, a dog or a tiger.
Lina: I could be a cat, I have got a cat, she is quite fast.
Peter: We do not discuss 'fast', we discuss 'wise'!
            Henning: We are discussing fast as well, I mean being 'fast in thinking'.
Peter: But animals cannot think.

Florian:	Of course they can. They know perfectly well who is coming home. If they do not know you, they bark. If they know you, they bark as well, but their barking sounds different. So they know who is coming.
Teacher:	Is the story about the question whether or not animals can think?
Florian:	Yes, it is.
Sabrina:	No, it is not.
Henning:	They are just playing animals, they are not really animals. They are playing the way they imagine animals to be.
Teacher:	Do you think animals are not as Till and Mary imagine them to be?
Henning:	Animals may well be how Till and Mary expect them to be, but the animals do not exactly know about that. The turtle may be slow, but may be wise at the same time.
Sabrina:	But if you are slow in thinking, you won't finish your work in time and won't get the number of points needed and eventually get a bad mark.
Hannes:	I never manage to finish my work.
Bernd:	Nor do I.
Henrike:	We should always have time enough to finish.
Henning:	If so, I will always have to wait for the others. I think everybody must be able to finish quickly.
Teacher:	What must we be able to do quickly?
Henning:	We must be quick at calculating.
Maximilian:	And also at writing.
Teacher:	Might it sometimes be good to do a thing slowly?
Henrike:	It's all the same if you think slowly or quickly, the main thing is that you get correct results. And if someone has finished, he will be free to do something else.
Laura:	Puzzles must be done slowly, otherwise it won't work.

Till so far.

The Second Variant

This one starts with examples given by a group of children about 'friendship':

196

Stefanie:	When I was playing with my brother, his friends rang the bell.
	He simply left me alone and went out.
Johann:	After our training Jacob and I went to our neighbour. We were playing on the computer. I was not so good at that. That's why they started cracking jokes about me. When I told them to stop, they did not. I found them rude.
Jacob:	At Easter an egg had been hidden in a tree. I wanted to get it and fell down, injuring my foot. Jan took that chance and took the egg away.

So far the children's examples. The children were then asked to chose one example for a dialogue, and chose Johann's. The dialogue lasted for one hour. The children narrated what they had been through. They compared their own experiences with Johann's example. They arrived at a common opinion on the following statements:

> Jokes by a friend can hurt badly.
> Jokes will always hurt if you cannot fight back.

In a meta-discussion one child asked the other children to evaluate the dialogue about Johann's example, to find out whether or not it was a good dialogue. In a strategy talk which followed, two questions were formulated and it was decided to start the next lesson with these questions:

> Why was Johann unable to fight back?
> Why did Johann's friends behave like that?

Concluding Thoughts

During the second variant the usual structure of the Socratic Dialogue was followed (division of the process into content, meta and strategy dialogue). This meant that the children worked not merely on the content of a given problem, but also reflected about their own behaviour and the subjective feelings experienced by dialogue participants.

All children participated enthusiastically in both the described dialogues, as described above. They felt they were taken seriously and were not overstretched as one might think. By way of summary, I would like to emphasize the following points:

- The starting point of a dialogue must be something which encourages the children to reflect;
- The subject-matter can be almost anything, but certain constraints and structures are necessary;
- The children start with their own concrete experience;
- 'Free speech' reigns;
- The children test their thoughts in interaction with those of their classmates;
- The dialogue's evolvement, as far as possible, is determined by the children;
- Different viewpoints alongside each other are accepted; as far as possible no judgments are made;
- The facilitator's (i.e. the teacher's) role is to encourage and co-ordinate;
- The aim is to seek reasons in support of opinions, but the children are not obliged to give reasons;
- Questions left open are formulated at the end of the lesson.

In my view such dialogues contribute to encouraging children's capacities to communicate and to reflect. For this reason they should already be practised during the primary phase in school.

Rene Saran

Socratic Dialogue on "When is unequal treatment acceptable?"[1]

Rationale for Topic

The ideal of equality acclaimed by the French Revolution has a high value for Rene Saran. She has often observed that in practice individuals, communities, local authorities and the state treat people unequally with the intention to give them an 'equal chance'. In Britain this has been referred to as 'positive discrimination' or, more recently, as 'social inclusion', so that disadvantaged members of society are enabled to participate in their community and society. In many countries policies have been developed to include children with a disability in mainstream rather than in segregated schools which cater for special educational needs (e.g. for the deaf, blind, behaviourally disturbed). This was the background to Rene formulating the question "*When is unequal treatment acceptable?*"

The Group's Examples

The group, as usual, commenced with participants giving their personally experienced examples. They included the following:

- *A doctor sponsored expensive treatment for one child because the parents exerted pressure and the doctor favoured the research opportunity.*

---

1   Report on SD Group. Facilitator: Rene Saran..Group: 8 Participants (5 German, 3 Japanese).

- *On a train an old man and an old woman were without a seat. There was no difference between them except gender. A young man gave his seat to the woman, but was unsure whether he would do so again.*
- *After a male student had been attacked, another student was asked to warn especially women not to walk alone at night. He did not want to treat women unequally, so he informed all students about the attack.*
- *A woman student experienced as humiliating the unequal treatment of lesbian (compared with heterosexual) couples by university admission regulations.*
- *A newly qualified teacher treated a talented boy equally with other pupils, but outside the class made special efforts on his behalf. He thought this action acceptable, but felt uncertain about his efforts in respect of talents possessed by other pupils.*

The last example was chosen by the group.

The chosen Example in full

As a second year probationary teacher I was working in a school in a rural area. I taught different subjects in different classes. In one class there was an eleven-year old boy (Thomas) who was really interested in my subject — history. After lessons he talked to me and it was clear that he already had a lot of knowledge although he could not always express his ideas and knowledge clearly. When I looked at the mark sheet I found he had only average marks. The boy was also eagerly interested in several other subjects.

I decided to support Thomas by buying books for which he paid. (I also bought books for others). I became aware that Thomas was not fully stretched in that school and thought he would develop better if he went to a grammar school. On asking him I found out he was eager to attend a boarding grammar school, already attended by some of his friends. His mother was unsure whether a grammar school was the best for him and I tried to convince her to let her son go. He did go. The class teacher did not agree with my judgement, and told me this later. It was clear to me (even at that time) that I treated Thomas differently (unequally) from the other pupils. My action was acceptable to me because I wanted to foster Thomas' talents because otherwise they might have gone under. I still take this view. Today I wonder whether I gave sufficient attention to the other pupils. I did more for Thomas than I did for the others.

Distinction between different and unequal treatment

The example-giver ended his outline with the question:

Was my treatment of Thomas unequal?

Participants offered a range of answers which introduced the distinction between 'different' and 'unequal' treatment. At the same time judgements were made about the acceptability of the teacher's action.

- *The special treatment of Thomas was acceptable. Different treatments are in themselves not unequal treatments, but lack of attention to the other children would mean to treat them unequally, which is not acceptable. In one sentence: unequal treatment can be or may be acceptable;*
- *(agreeing with the above) Each pupil has the right to be treated differently but not to be treated unequally;*
- *The teacher treated Thomas differently and unequally. It is difficult to distinguish between 'different' and 'unequal'. The teacher's action was adequate;*
- *If the different treatment of Thomas arose out of the teacher's appreciation of all pupils having equal rights then his action is acceptable.*

The above range of views led to the next question addressed by the group:

What, then, is the difference between 'different' and 'unequal' treatment in the example?

This was approached by a participant in a three-part statement:

(1) In order to foster the special potential of a single pupil (Thomas), it required the teacher to treat him differently from the other;

(2) Every pupil has two rights:
a) that the teacher notices his potential
b)that the teacher fosters his potential;

(3) If the teacher did not do his best to notice and foster the potential of all pupils in different (and therefore adequate) ways, then the treatment of Thomas was unequal and not acceptable.

The example-giver added:

I went beyond treating Thomas differently. By 'beyond' I want to explain that: I looked for books; spoke to mother; gave time after lessons; encouraged Thomas to go to grammar school. For me this was unequal treatment and acceptable.

Another participant immediately disagreed:

The treatment was unequal and not acceptable.

After these answers, the group established that six participants thought the teacher's action was *unequal treatment* of Thomas, five of whom found it acceptable, one unacceptable. However, the two remaining participants argued that the example was *not one involving unequal treatment.*

Formulation of Reasons

In an attempt to resolve the above differences group members agreed to marshal their thoughts *why* the teacher's action towards Thomas was either acceptable or unacceptable, or did not involve unequal treatment.

A. Why the Action was acceptable

(4)   When a young pupil shows talent, the teacher should foster it;
(5)   In the example, the teacher noticed and fostered Thomas' talents;

Thomas was growing up in a non-supportive environment (rural school, parent's attitude etc) and his chances without support would have been very limited;
(6)   *The teacher did not ignore the other children.*

B. Why the Action was unacceptable

The reason for this view was formulated in terms of the expectations we have of teachers:

An ideal teacher should be neutral towards all pupils in a class because all are equal in value, although different in talents. To single out one pupil for special support is treating that pupil unequally and that is unacceptable because it will disturb the class (or group) of equal pupils.

C. Why the Action did not involve unequal treatment

The teacher's action was the beginning of a process towards fuller equality and from the start it was not really unequal treatment, and it was acceptable. Unequal treatment (as described above by the example-giver) in a particular case is acceptable only if the action serves the purpose of more equality. The actor (in this case the teacher) has to take into account the views of the wider community in judging whether the action serves this wider purpose.

Comment by Facilitator

Progress of the group was necessarily slow as communication and mutual understanding in the English language proved difficult. The patience shown by group members was admirable and enabled us to work well and co-operatively together. This report demonstrates important aspects of the Socratic Dialogue: clear formulation of the chosen example; agreement on further questions to pursue; that initially the discussion kept closely to the concrete example; pursuit of emerging conceptual confusions (between the meaning of unequal and different); recording of judgements about the example (acceptability /unacceptability of the teacher's action); attempts to resolve conflicts of judgement. Towards the end, some broader, more general views were expressed (moving from the particular to the more general or abstract level).

Time constraints prevented the group from exploring these more abstract judgements which had arisen from the group's deepened understanding of the example and the exploration of the teacher's particular action.

Sokratisches Philosophieren

Schriftenreihe der
Philosophisch-Politischen Akademie
(PPA) und der Gesellschaft für
Sokratisches Philosophieren (GSP)
hrsg. von Dieter Krohn, Barbara Neißer,
Nora Walter †

Dieter Krohn; Barbara Neißer (Hg.)
Verständigung über Verständigung
Metagespräche über Sokratische Gespräche
Zur Methode des Sokratischen Gesprächs
gehört als unverzichtbarer Bestandteil die
Metakommunikation (Metagespräch.) Der
Band enthält Beiträge zu unterschiedlichen
Formen und Funktionen der Metakommu-
nikation über das Sokratischen Gespräch.
Verfahren und Bedeutung des teilnehmer-
orientierten Metagesprächs, des Analyse-
und Strategiegespräches stehen im Zentrum
der Darstellungen. Praxisberichte aus unter-
schiedlichen Anwendungsfeldern ergänzen
den thematischen Schwerpunkt des Bands.
Bd. 8, 2004, 232 S., 19,90 €, br.,
ISBN 3-8258-6300-x

Gisela Raupach-Strey
Sokratische Didaktik
Die didaktische Bedeutung der Sokratischen Methode in der Tradition von
Leonard Nelson und Gustav Heckmann
Sokratische Gespräche, wie sie seit den 20er
Jahren in der Tradition von Leonard Nelson
und Gustav Heckmann praktiziert werden,
enthalten einen die antiken Sokrates-Dialoge
nur partiell integrierenden Entwurf, den die
Autorin als „Sokratisches Paradigma" in sei-
nen konstitutiven Elementen darstellt, unter
philosophischen, fach- und allgemeindidak-
tischen Aspekten näher untersucht und dessen Stärken für den Philosophie- und Ethik-
Unterricht sowie diverse andere Lernkontexte
sie aufzeigt. Erfahrungsbezogenes Philosophieren, Überwindung von Sprachlosigkeit
und gedankliche Primärerfahrungen sind
unter gegenwärtigen gesellschaftlichen Bedingungen von nicht zu unterschätzender Bedeutung. Die Focussierung auf das Gespräch,
das im Kern auch andere Unterrichts- und
Lernformen durchdringt, stärkt das Selbst-
vertrauen in vernünftige Denktätigkeit und
die gegenseitige maieutische Denkhilfe in
einer Lerngemeinschaft. Schließlich werden
Reflexionen, Einblicke und Anregungen für
die Praxis Sokratischer Gespräche gegeben,
die vor allem in der Lehrerbildung ihr didakti-
sches Potential entfalten können.
Bd. 10, 2002, 656 S., 35,90 €, br.,
ISBN 3-8258-6322-0

Patricia Shipley; Heidi Mason (Eds.)
**Ethics and Socratic Dialogue in Civil
Society**
How can we build unity in an increasingly
divided world? Could new forms of dialogue
be used as a tool to foster understanding in
today's fragmented societies? This volume represents a concerted attempt to think through
the difficult and urgent issues facing civil
society today. It considers the potential role of dialogue, especially modern Socratic
Dialogue, to help answer some of the ethical
questions and issues that face us all. Itself a
result of international dialogue and collaboration, this book will be of interest to anyone
concerned about the role of civil society in
today's world.
Bd. 11, 2004, 240 S., 24,90 €, br.,
ISBN 3-8258-7925-9

Wissenschaftliche Paperbacks
Philosophie

Hans-Georg Gadamer
Die Lektion des Jahrhunderts
Ein philosophischer Dialog mit Riccar-
do Dottori
Gadamers Hermeneutik des suchenden Ge-
sprächs ermöglicht vielen Disziplinen der
Geistes- und Sozialwissenschaften, Wege
des fachlichen Erkennens mit historischen
Sichtweisen zu verknüpfen. Seit "Wahrheit
und Methode" (1960) rühmt man die von ihm
geleistete "Urbanisierung der Heideggerschen
Provinz" (Habermas). Versteht Gadamer jede

LIT Verlag Münster – Berlin – Hamburg – London – Wien
Grevener Str./Fresnostr. 2 48159 Münster
Tel.: 0251 – 62 032 22 – Fax: 0251 – 23 19 72
e-Mail: vertrieb@lit-verlag.de – http://www.lit-verlag.de

Aussage als Antwort auf eine Frage, so ist Leben als Dialog neu zu verstehen.
Bd. 2, 2. Aufl. 2003, 168 S., 15,90 €, br., ISBN 3-8258-5049-8; 34,90€, gb., ISBN 3-8258-5768-9

Hans Jonas
Fatalismus wäre Todsünde
Gespräche über Ethik und Mitverantwortung im dritten Jahrtausend. Herausgegeben von Dietrich Böhler im Auftrag des Hans Jonas-Zentrums e. V.
Hans Jonas konnte 1979, als Europa sich die Augen rieb und zu räsonieren begann, ob der technologisch industrielle Fortschritt eine "ökologische Krise" verursache, schon seine tiefdringende „Ethik der technologischen Zivilisation" vorlegen. Deren Grundgedanken und ihre Orientierung für das 21. Jahrhundert – das erste einer technologisch und wirtschaftlich "globalisierten" Menschheit – hat er in eindringlichen Gesprächen vor Augen geführt und im Blick auf künftige Entwicklungen zugespitzt. Gegen den Pessimismus macht er Mut zur Mitverantwortung, gegen die Augenblicksversessenheit erschließt er Orientierungssinn aus der jüdisch-christlichen Tradition. Der Berliner Ethiker Dietrich Böhler, der auch die LIT-Reihe „Ethik und Wirtschaft im Dialog" mitherausgibt, hat besonders aussagekräftige, aber kaum mehr greifbare, Gespräche zusammengestellt. Einführend gibt er einen Einblick in die Stationen von Jonas' Denken; zum aktuellen Schluß kontrastiert er PID und Embryonen 'verbrauchende' Forschung mit den Prinzipien Verantwortung und Menschenwürde.
Bd. 19, 2005, 224 S., 17,90 €, br., ISBN 3-8258-7573-3

Philosophie: Forschung und Wissenschaft

Hubertus Mynarek
Mystik und Vernunft
Das Buch ist in jedem seiner zahlreichen Kapitel der Beweis für die These, dass ohne Aufklärung, ohne Vernunft jede Mystik, jede Spiritualität und Religiosität blind und dumm wird, dass aber umgekehrt ohne Mystik und Spiritualität jede Aufklärung, jede Art von Vernunfterkenntnis flach, eng und schwachbrüstig, trocken und leblos, ja oft lebenszerstörend und menschenvernichtend wirkt. Deshalb stellt dieses Buch den großangelegten Versuch dar, die beiden für echtes menschliches Leben absolut notwendigen, scheinbar gegensätzlichen Pole – Mystik und Vernunft – einer tragfähigen und fruchtbaren Synthese zuzuführen. Der Autor – Philosoph, Theologe, Religionswissenschaftler – erarbeitet seine weit ausgreifenden, grenzüberschreitenden, den herkömmlichen Wissenschafts- und Vernunftbegriff erweiternden Perspektiven vor allem auf der Basis der Psycho- und Sozioanalyse, der Physik, der Technik und Technokratie sowie der Phänomenanalyse von Angst und Glauben. Mit diesem Werk werden die Türen für geistiges Neuland, für neue Ideen, für mentale Originalität und Kreativität weit aufgestoßen.
Bd. 1, 2. überarb. u. erw. Auflage 2001, 264 S., 20,90 €, br., ISBN 3-8258-5312-8

Klaus Kornwachs
Logik der Zeit – Zeit der Logik
Eine Einführung in die Zeitphilosophie. Anhang mit Aufgaben/Lösungen
Der Versuch, Zeit zu verstehen, ist ein altes Problem der Philosophie. Zeiterfahrung und Zeitverständnis spielen sich auf mehreren unterschiedlichen Ebenen ab und man kann sich einem Zeitverständnis auf vielerlei Wegen zu nähern versuchen, nicht zuletzt durch genaue Beobachtung der eigenen Zeitwahrnehmung. Die – geistesgeschichtlich gesehen – jungen Naturwissenschaften haben viele neue Bausteine zu einem Zeitverständnis beigetragen und die Hilfsmittel hierfür sind immer abstrakter geworden. Eine Lösung der philosophischen Fragen nach Grund, Wesen und innerer Struktur der Zeit konnten auch sie noch nicht liefern.
Bd. 2, 2001, 424 S., 35,90 €, br., ISBN 3-8258-4787-x

LIT Verlag Münster – Berlin – Hamburg – London – Wien
Grevener Str./Fresnostr. 2 48159 Münster
Tel.: 0251 – 62 032 22 – Fax: 0251 – 23 19 72
e-Mail: vertrieb@lit-verlag.de – http://www.lit-verlag.de

Norbert Kapferer
Die Nazifizierung der Philosophie an der Universität Breslau 1933–1945
Dem Schicksal der Philosophie an der Universität Breslau zwischen 1933 und 1945 widmet sich die auf Archivmaterial gestützte Arbeit Kapferers. Der Autor rekonstruiert den Verlauf der "Nazifizierung" und die damit einhergehende Zerschlagung einer durch jüdische Denker geprägten philosophischen Kultur. Ins Blickfeld geraten die Aktivitäten von NS-Organisationen und Hochschulinstitutionen wie die Initiativen von Rektoren, Dekanen, Direktoren und Professoren aus Breslau und anderen deutschen Universitätsstädten. Es begegnen sehr bekannte Namen wie Heidegger, Litt, Bollnow, Rothacker, Alfred Baeumler, Ernst Krieck etc. und längst in Vergessenheit geratene NS-Philosophen wie Karl Bornhausen (Redner bei der Bücherverbrennung) und August Faust (Sprachrohr des "Amtes Rosenberg" und Verfasser einer Philosophie des "totalen Krieges"). Deutlich wird, dass die nazifizierte Philosophie in Breslau unter der Führung von Faust eine nicht unbedeutende Rolle in der Universitätslandschaft des "III. Reiches" spielte. Eine exemplarische Studie zur "Machtergreifung".
Bd. 3, 2002, 272 S., 45,90 €, br.,
ISBN 3-8258-5451-5

Walter Schweidler
Das Unantastbare
Beiträge zur Philosophie der Menschenrechte
Würde und Rechte des Menschen: Mit diesen Begriffen bezeichnen wir das Verhältnis, aufgrund dessen sich die menschlichen von allen nichtmenschlichen Wesen unterscheiden. An der vernünftigen Verständigung über die Bedingungen der Aufrechterhaltung dieses Verhältnisses entscheiden sich die Konsistenz unserer Rechtssysteme, die interkulturelle Vermittelbarkeit unterschiedlicher Vorstellungen von Humanität und die Möglichkeiten des Brückenschlages zwischen Ethik und Politik.
Bd. 5, 2001, 264 S., 30,90 €, gb.,
ISBN 3-8258-5724-7

Harald Holz
Bewußtsein und Gehirn, eine philosophische Metareflexion
Erkenntnistheoretische und forschungslogische Erwägungen im Voraus zur einzelwissenschaftlichen Problemlage
In diesem Buch wird der Versuch unternommen, die hochkomplexe Problematik dessen, was heute unter dem Stichwort "Gehirn-Bewußtseins-Beziehung" behandelt wird, von einem neuen Denkansatz aus zu verstehen. Alle bisherigen Deutungen gingen entweder von einem monistischen oder aber von einem interaktionistischen Schema aus. Wird im ersten Fall der Begriff "Geist" auf materiale Bedingungen reduziert, so fristet im zweiten Fall dies "Geistige" eine merkwürdige Sonderexistenz von ähnlich gegenständlicher Natur wie das Materielle selbst, nur auf höherer Ebene. – Hier nun wird die Logik des "Entweder – Oder" aufgehoben zugunsten einer Sicht, die beide bisher als einander ausschließend gedachten Pole als Extremmomente eines in sich selber kontinuierlichen dynamischen Ganzen zu denken erlaubt. Das maßgebende Modell hierfür wurde vermittels einer entsprechenden philosophischen Analyse der Methode beim Aufbau der Funktionalstruktur des Infinitesimalkalküls gefunden. – Die so gewonnene Perspektive erlaubt, Gehirnaktivität und Reflexionsbewußtsein als Extreme eines Kontinuums, sofern man menschliche Wesenheit als solches auffaßt, zu deuten, zugleich aber dennoch dem Geist-Pol ein irreduzibles Eigengewicht zuzubilligen.
Bd. 6, 2001, 192 S., 20,90 €, br.,
ISBN 3-8258-5780-8

Theodor Leiber
Natur-Ethik, Verantwortung und Universalmoral
Es werden die Grundregeln einer universalisierbaren archekakopheugischen Minimalmoral formuliert, deren anthropozentrische Ausgangskonzeption in der Natur-Ethik systematisch auf die moralischen Probleme unseres Umgangs mit der (außermenschlichen) Natur ausgedehnt wird. Die entsprechenden anthropophysio-relationalen uni-

LIT Verlag Münster – Berlin – Hamburg – London – Wien
Grevener Str./Fresnostr. 2 48159 Münster
Tel.: 0251 – 62 032 22 – Fax: 0251 – 23 19 72
e-Mail: vertrieb@lit-verlag.de – http://www.lit-verlag.de

versalmoralischen Grundregeln bilden die Basis für einen modifizierten Grundrechtskatalog und dienen als Kriterien, um die in der zeitgenössischen Natur-Ethik vertretenen Naturschutzargumente auf ihre universalmoralische Verbindlichkeit hin zu überprüfen und daraus unterstützende Hinweise für eine Naturschutz-Pädagogik zu gewinnen.
Bd. 7, 2002, 296 S., 24,80 €, br.,
ISBN 3-8258-5368-3

Uwe Bernhardt; Friederike Denker; Hans Martin Dober (Hg.)
Rolf Denker: Hiob – oder die Schwere des Glücks
Ein philosophisches Lesebuch über Leben und Lebenlassen
In den hier versammelten Reden und Aufsätzen setzt sich ein Weisheits-Liebender mit der Bibel ebenso auseinander wie mit Kafka, ein Weisheits-Lehrer wagt sich an eine Deutung des Expressionismus ebenso wie an eine Interpretation der Träume Descartes'. Zwei Leitfragen ziehen sich wie Fäden durch das Gewebe dieser Texte. Die eine betrifft das erfahrene Leid. Deshalb ist auch dem Buch Hiob die Konstellation abzulesen, in der diese Beiträge ihren Zusammenhang finden. Die andere Frage betrifft das Verhältnis zum anderen Menschen. Eine mit Levinas radikal gefasste Ethik ist in diesem Band ebenso präsent wie der kulturtheoretische Anspruch der Psychoanalyse. Stets wird dabei die philosophische Anthropologie, wie Rolf Denker sie vertritt, auf die geschichtsphilosophische Signatur bezogen, in der die conditio humana ihre jeweilige Konkretion gewinnt.
Bd. 8, 2002, 152 S., 17,90 €, br.,
ISBN 3-8258-5990-8

Peter Gottwald
Zen im Westen – neue Lehrrede für eine alte Übung
Das Buch wendet sich an alle, die von der Zen – Lehre gehört haben, davon fasziniert sind und sich fragen, wie eine Integration dieser aus dem Buddhismus kommenden Tradition in die westliche wissenschaftlich-technische Welt möglich ist. Sein Schwerpunkt liegt in der Formulierung einer entsprechenden Lehrrede, seine Suche gilt darüber hinaus einer neuen Kultur. Das Buch zeigt Verbindungslinien auf zwischen der Zentradition und der Mystik, der Philosophie, der Psychologie, der Soziologie, der Psychiatrie, modernen erkenntnistheoretischen Versuchen und zum religiösen Bereich. Es geht um die gegenwärtige Möglichkeit, frei ein neues „Miteinander" zu üben.
Bd. 9, 2003, 224 S., 19,90 €, br.,
ISBN 3-8258-6734-x

Friedrich Rapp
Destruktive Freiheit
Ein Plädoyer gegen die Maßlosigkeit der modernen Welt
Charakteristisch für die moderne Welt ist der Wille zur Innovation. Auf dem Gebiet der Kultur ebenso wie in der Sphäre der Gesellschaft und der Technik wird die Aufhebung von Schranken und das Überschreiten von Grenzen als höchste Errungenschaft gefeiert. Doch dieses maßlose Freiheitsstreben stellt nicht nur eine Bereicherung und einen Fortschritt dar, es führt auch zum Verlust an Orientierung und Strukturierung und im Grenzfall zum Chaos. Im Sinne dieser These untersucht der Autor die theoretischen Prämissen, die zur gegenwärtigen Situation geführt haben, und diskutiert mögliche Anknüpfungspunkte für einen Wandel.
Bd. 10, 2004, 232 S., 17,90 €, br.,
ISBN 3-8258-7126-6

Christian Lavagno
Rekonstruktion der Moderne
Eine Studie zu Habermas und Foucault
Das Buch unternimmt den Versuch einer Rekonstruktion des philosophischen Diskurses der Moderne. Grundlage sind zwei bereits vorliegende (und konkurrierende) Entwürfe zu diesem Thema, der eine von Jürgen Habermas, der andere von Michel Foucault. Diese beiden Entwürfe werden sowohl für sich kritisch betrachtet als auch vergleichend gegenübergestellt. Am Ende des Vergleichs kristallisiert sich eine übergreifende Bestimmung der modernen Philosophie heraus, die – so der Anspruch des Buches – unabhängig

LIT Verlag Münster – Berlin – Hamburg – London – Wien
Grevener Str./Fresnostr. 2 48159 Münster
Tel.: 0251 – 62 032 22 – Fax: 0251 – 23 19 72
e-Mail: vertrieb@lit-verlag.de – http://www.lit-verlag.de

von den verschiedenen Schulen den Kern modernen philosophischen Denkens freilegt.
Bd. 11, 2003, 272 S., 29,90 €, br.,
ISBN 3-8258-7173-8

Michael Sukale; Stefan Treitz (Hg..)
Philosophie und Bewegung
Interdisziplinäre Betrachtungen
Dieses Buch umfasst eine Reihe von Beiträgen, deren Autoren aus verschiedenen wissenschaftlichen und philosophischen Perspektiven heraus über die menschliche Bewegung – vor allem am Beispiel von Sportbewegungen – nachdenken. Verbunden sind die – teilweise gegensätzlichen – Aufsätze durch dokumentierte Diskussionen, die sich im Auditorium eines gemeinsamen Forschungsseminares entwickelten. Es kommen Philosophen, Sportwissenschaftler, Soziologen, Pädagogen, Psychologen und Bewegungswissenschaftler zu Wort, die sich die Aufgabe gestellt haben in diesem Rahmen nach einem philosophischen Verständnis der menschlichen Bewegung zu suchen.
Bd. 12, 2004, 328 S., 24,90 €, br.,
ISBN 3-8258-7704-3

J. C. Horn
Hegel besser verstehen
Das ignorierte Prinzip
Kant, „der größte deutsche Philosoph"? Dabei wird übersehen, bei Kants Tod war bereits ein Größerer am Werk: Hegel, der Philosoph des Werdens und der Entwicklung. – Kant wurde halbwegs verstanden, Hegel gar nicht. Also wird hier der Versuch vorgelegt, ihn wenigstens etwas zu verstehen. Der Bogen versuchten Verstehens beginnt bei Leibniz, geht über Kant, Fichte und Schelling weiter, wobei die Erfahrungen von Freud und Jung etwas mehr als Fußnoten abgeben. Kant hat die Welt der Vorstellung ausgemessen. Hegel hat die geschichtliche Welt als denkendes Leben begriffen, welches – über Verkehrung und Tod hinaus – den Atem der Seele betreibt.
Bd. 13, 2005, 432 S., 39,90 €, br.,
ISBN 3-8258-7316-1

Elmar Waibl
Grundriß der Medizinethik für Ärzte, Pflegeberufe und Laien
Humanversuch, Tierexperiment, Gentechnik, Reproduktionsmedizin, Schwangerschaftsabbruch, Transplantationsmedizin, Gesundheitsökonomie, Suizid, Sterbehilfe – die heiklen und irritierenden Fragen der Medizinethik gehen buchstäblich „unter die Haut". Entsprechend kontrovers verläuft die gesellschaftliche Auseinandersetzung mit diesen Themen. In übersichtlicher und verständlicher Weise vermittelt das vorliegende Buch dem Leser alle Voraussetzungen, sich kompetent und kritisch an der Diskussion zu beteiligen. Zugespitzte Pro- und Contra-Gegenüberstellung erleichtern die Orientierung in schwierigen Entscheidungsfragen, die uns alle bedrängen.
Bd. 14, 2004, 304 S., 17,90 €, br.,
ISBN 3-8258-7521-0

H. Baum
Theorien sozialer Gerechtigkeit
Politische Philosophie für soziale Berufe
Bd. 15, 2004, 184 S., 24,90 €, br.,
ISBN 3-8258-7752-3

Walfried Linden; Alfred Fleissner (Hg.)
Geist, Seele und Gehirn
Entwurf eines gemeinsamen Menschenbildes von Neurobiologen und Geisteswissenschaftlern
Bd. 16, 2004, 216 S., 14,90 €, br.,
ISBN 3-8258-7973-9

Kurt Salamun (Hg.)
Fundamentalismus „interdisziplinär"
Bd. 19, 2005, 360 S., 17,90 €, br.,
ISBN 3-8258-7621-7

Renate Dürr; Gunter Gebauer;
Matthias Maring Hans-Peter Schütt(Hg.)
Pragmatisches Philosophieren
Festschrift für Hans Lenk
Bd. 20, 2005, 464 S., 39,90 €, br.,
ISBN 3-8258-7131-2

LIT Verlag Münster – Berlin – Hamburg – London – Wien
Grevener Str./Fresnostr. 2 48159 Münster
Tel.: 0251 – 62 032 22 – Fax: 0251 – 23 19 72
e-Mail: vertrieb@lit-verlag.de – http://www.lit-verlag.de